ART CLOTH

A GUIDE TO
SURFACE DESIGN FOR FABRIC

JANE DUNNEWOLD

Editors: Elaine Lipson, Linda Griepentrog
Art Director: Liz Quan
Cover and interior design: Lee Calderon
Photography: Joe Coca
Photography pages 151–153: Brent Kane
Production design: Katherine Jackson

Interweave Press LLC
201 East Fourth Street
Loveland, CO 80537
interweavestore.com

Printed in China by Asia Pacific Offset, Ltd.

Library of Congress Cataloging-in-Publication Data

Dunnewold, Jane, 1954-
  Art cloth : a guide to surface design for fabric / Jane Dunnewold.
      p. cm.
  Includes bibliographical references and index.
  ISBN 978-1-59668-195-8
  1. Textile crafts. 2. Textile design. 3. Textile finishing. I. Title.
  TT699.D83 2010
  746–dc22
                              2010002777

10 9 8 7 6 5 4 3 2 1

Art cloth by Kathleen McTee, made with fiber-reactive dyes, discharge methods, and foil.

DEDICATION

To my favorite students everywhere.

ACKNOWLEDGMENTS

I am grateful for the help I received from thoughtful and talented writers and editors—Tricia Waddell, Linda Griepentrog, and Elaine Lipson. And also for the professional handling and photography provided by Interweave's talented artists.

Thanks to colleagues and students who were willing to share their samples and creative impulse with my readers.

And special thanks to my sisters, Ann, Ruth, and Mary; my mother, Elinor; and my daughter, Zenna, each of whom buoys and inspires me. I am incredibly fortunate to share this lifetime with them.

contents

Jane Dunnewold, 2008.
Silk with fiber-reactive dye, soy-wax resist, hand coloring, pencil.

introduction

In 1994, I woke up at four in the morning with the term "complex cloth" floating in my head. Little did I know how that epiphany would change my life. The term married together all of the printing and dyeing processes I'd been studying and gave me a structure to combine them. Thousands of yards later, complex cloth has evolved into *art cloth*—an art form understood and practiced by artists all over the globe.

This book is my opportunity to share art cloth with you. Not only have I produced thousands of yards of fabric, I've been privileged to work with about a thousand students over the years since 1994. While I love dyeing and printing cloth, and the endless surprises that rise up from the printing table, I love more the delight and enthusiasm I witness in students when the process touches them in a way that often defies description. Who would have thought that *making* could change a life?

But *making* changed my life. At loose ends for the first twenty years of my adult life, *making* became my daily practice. Studio time is a creative gift we give ourselves, but it is also a meditation that can take us deep into ourselves, and if we are determined and rigorous, out the other side to balance and mental health. That's what *making* has done for me.

I see it in workshops all the time. We live in a culture where we aren't always honored as creative spirits and where personal ability is often dis-counted. But put twelve people in a classroom with a dye bucket and a few printing tools, announce that the inner critic must sit quietly and isn't allowed to play in this space, and edges soften. Ideas blossom. *Making* reigns supreme. It's not that frustrations can't arise—of course they do. I wrote this book because of what I know from all of those workshops. No one needs to reinvent the wheel; I can help.

You hold in your hands my best shot at sharing reliable processes with you. I hope you'll read this, acquire a few supplies, and begin. Art cloth can be anything, but a great place to start is with the layering process. Perhaps as you add layers to your cloth, you'll peel back a few about yourself. There is a rich opportunity to discover yourself through *making*.

Whether you work through this book cover to cover, or skim it prior to delving in, take seriously the challenge to make your work your own. The information is the foundation for you to build upon. Study it, work with it to master the techniques, and then add your own personal brand to the processes. Mix them up and combine them with other skills you already possess. No one will use the same images you invent and no one will combine processes in exactly the same way you combine them.

Be safe. Be careful, and strive to reflect who you are through the practice of making cloth. And let me know how it's going.

Jane Dunnewold

Paradise I, Jane Dunnewold, 2005.
Silk organza with silkscreened textile paint, handpainted thickened dyes, gold metallic paint printed with Thermofax screen, and gold leaf.

work space, tools, and materials

This book is designed to help you explore the infinite possibilities of art cloth. Most of us are eager to begin to manifest the designs we imagine. But first, you must have a reasonably methodical approach to trying out different methods and recording the results of your experiments, and a safe, comfortable, and appropriately equipped work space. This chapter offers my best pointers for creating a working environment that will allow your artistic vision to flourish.

Safety and Environmental Awareness :: Setting Up Your Work Space :: Tools and Supplies
Fabrics :: Making Samples and Keeping Records

A selection of dyed fabrics ready to become art cloth.

FIRST THINGS FIRST: SAFETY AND ENVIRONMENTAL AWARENESS

When it comes to the nuts and bolts of making art cloth, you must make safety a priority. Actually wear your gloves and mask. Put buying a comfortable respirator first on your shopping list. Think twice before being seduced by chemical processes you can't possibly conduct safely in a home environment. Just because you can, doesn't mean you should! Safety tips for dyeing and discharging are detailed in Chapters 3 and 4, respectively.

And while you're at it, be judicious in your approach to environmental waste. Thrift stores are filled with stuff that can be adapted to studio use. You aren't cooking in there. Use old electric skillets and tableware and all manner of other cast-off things as inexpensive outfitting for your very practical space.

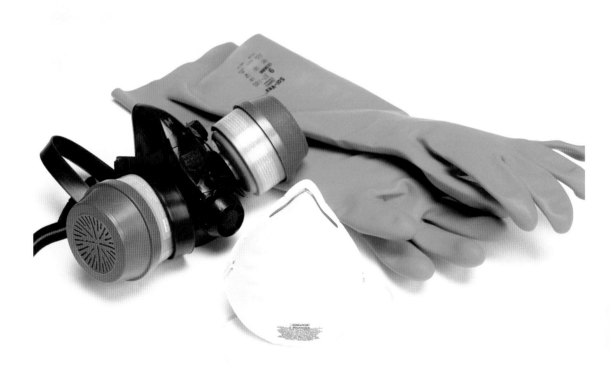

Respirators and gloves are important for safety.

ART CLOTH

SETTING UP YOUR WORK SPACE

Setting up a work area is important. We all have different circumstances. Some folks have the luxury of a large dedicated space. Others have limited resources, space, and time. However it is, we make do with what we have. In the beginning, you won't know exactly what you need when it comes to time, space, and equipment anyway, so try to enjoy the process of figuring it out.

It's a luxury to have a space you don't have to clean up or one you can totally cover with plastic. It's distracting to worry about the floor and spills. You may not have a space dedicated to a studio. If you don't, try to carve out work time of at least a few hours, or two days back to back. It's an efficient use of time, and you won't spend more time cleaning up and putting things away than you do working.

Prioritize studio needs and acquire things as time and money permit. Hot and cold running water and a cart to transfer supplies back and forth from the storage space to the workroom are real conveniences. A washer and dryer are helpful, and probably essential if you intend to print longer lengths of fabric. Good lighting is imperative. Consider color-corrected bulbs or Ott lights to facilitate accurate color selection and reproduction.

The lovely reality is that setting up is easier than it used to be because of our desire to work environmentally consciously. Less water, less dye, and smaller tools translate into an easier go of it when you are blissfully dyeing or printing away. Try not to get too caught up on what you don't have and focus instead on what you know and what you want to do. Desire is a powerful resource and overcomes incredible odds.

making a padded surface

A padded printing surface is a requirement. It doesn't have to be huge. A piece of plywood is fine, even if it's only two by three feet. I stretch two layers of felt over the plywood and staple it around the edges. Look for Kunin's Eco-Fi felt, made from recycled plastic bottles, and support an environmentally friendly product.

Brightly colored felt complicates seeing paint colors accurately. Choose a neutral color such as white or beige. Pull the felt tight when stapling it over the board and put the staples on the underside. A double felt surface isn't too soft that it would make it difficult to print fine detail but is padded and absorbent enough to make crisp, clean printing possible. Cover it with an old sheet each time you print and then wash the sheet at the end of the session. The sheet protects the felt and is easily washed and reused.

making a design wall

A design wall is a must. It can be as simple as a closet door covered with stick-on cork squares. I use metal boards from IKEA and heavy-duty magnets. A friend found a magnetic glue-on surface through the Internet and covered a whole wall in her studio with it. The important thing is to be able to stand back from your work. Looking down at fabric on a table is quite different from looking at it from across the room. Distance encourages you to see the bigger picture.

TOOLS AND SUPPLIES

stocking your supply cabinet

Acquiring tools and supplies is akin to a scavenger hunt. The Internet has revolutionized shopping, but many of us still want to support local businesses. Achieve a workable balance by doing both. Shopping locally offers a real-time *browse* factor because you can wander the aisles and encounter tools and/or ideas about how to adapt tools that might not occur if you were browsing online. On the other hand, shopping on the Internet allows you to compare prices, read up on new products that aren't sold by local stores, and shop in your pajamas at midnight if you are so inclined.

Everyone appreciates an opportunity to save money, but make sure you aren't compromising quality just to save a few bucks. Become familiar with suppliers and choose quality materials.

Dyes and paints are sold in several sizes. Buy small quantities the first time, so money won't be wasted on a dye color or paint type you'll never use up. Few of us need a pound of Bubblegum Pink dye. Just because it was on sale doesn't mean it was a smart purchase! On the other hand, some colors are the backbone of studio work, and buying those in quantity or when they are on sale makes good studio sense.

That old adage about the right tool for the job definitely applies to studio supplies. Shop thrift stores for equipment that can be adapted to studio use. Storage containers, mixing bowls, electric hot plates or skillets, and other miscellaneous items are as useful secondhand as they were new. Shop with an eye to value in a secondhand store and put the savings toward a really good steam iron or color-corrected light.

Label every chemical you acquire as soon as it enters the studio. I cut labels out of plastic packaging and tape them permanently to glass or plastic storage jars. Then I have not only the name of the product at my fingertips but also instructions for safe handling and use.

Online lists can be great resources. Members write frequently about new products and good deals they've found. The atmosphere is educational and sharing. Examples of open lists that welcome new members are included in Resources on page 173. Return the favor and share your discoveries, too; everyone wins.

A selection of supplies.

FABRICS

The art cloth you produce is only as good as the fabric you choose as the foundation. With this in mind, allow several factors to guide your fabric selection.

Most of the fabric in a fabric store is treated with sizing, which inhibits dye reaction and compromises color, so always pre-wash fabric before any dyeing or printing begins. Fabric that is labeled as Prepared for Dyeing (PFD) is a good choice, but even PFD cloth should be pre-washed. I use a half-cup of soda ash to pre-wash fabric in the washer, but you could use an additive-free laundry detergent, such as All Free and Clear. And yes, silk can be pre-washed using either of the above methods.

The dyes and discharging agents discussed in this book are formulated for natural fibers. Cellulose fibers (from plants) include cotton, linen, hemp, and rayon, or blends of those fibers. Protein fibers, such as silk and wool, are also compatible with the dyes and most of the discharging agents discussed.

If in doubt about fiber content, do a burn test. I keep a test kit in the car, with matches, a metal can lid, and a tiny bottle of bleach. Light a corner of a small sample. If it burns to a hard bead, it is synthetic. If it burns to an ash and/or smells like singed hair, the fabric is natural fiber. If you intend to discharge the fabric with bleach (cellulose fibers only, please) dab a bit of bleach on the cloth to determine its dischargeability.

The weave structure of the cloth affects the printed outcome. Smooth fabric is easier to print than textured fabric. Fabric with a pile, such as silk/rayon velvet, isn't a good choice for most

Prepared for Dyeing (PFD) fabrics are free of sizing.

printed applications. It dyes beautifully, but the pile disrupts a printed image and techniques such as foiling or printed paint are at cross-purposes with the beauty of the pile. If you want to work on a fabric with a challenging texture or pile, choose to work *with* the intrinsic nature of the cloth, rather than forcing it to become something it's not.

Many techniques are wonderful on dark or colored backgrounds, but in the interest of controlling variables, consider dyeing the fabric rather than starting with an unknown dye or pre-determined color palette. In the dance between control and serendipity, the wise artist discovers when to lead and when to follow. Explore these pages, techniques, and possibilities and enjoy the unique unfolding of your own *art cloth* path.

MAKING SAMPLES AND KEEPING RECORDS

I believe in the value of samples. When I teach a workshop, I always encourage participants to make samples of every process or technique they learn, even when it isn't appealing to them personally. You never know when you'll want to remember how you did a particular thing, and if you are like me, a visual record is always easier to figure out than written instructions. (Some students who've watched me try to unravel what I did from a sparse set of notes are probably laughing at this point!)

So consider your first challenge to be filling your "toolbox," or mastering technique. If you read these pages from start to finish and then return to them with the goal of making samples of the processes I've described, you'll have a valuable visual guide to each technique, and you'll be ready to make the work your own.

notebook

A notebook is a useful companion. Taking notes, even basic notations on processes and materials, means the difference between replicating a design you love a second time and wishing it were possible to do so. I'm not a notetaker myself, and I regularly regret it. Not having a notebook means flying by the seat of your pants and being satisfied with whatever your memory pieces together or serendipity offers. A reference notebook allows you to move more quickly through the learning stages of the creative process by limiting variables. It removes some of the guesswork. Cultivate notetaking as a habit.

Opposite: Dye samples.

Below: Dye sample notebook.

Fabric samples provide a visual record.

building layers

Art cloth features a series of dyed and printed layers, each contributing to the intricacy, beauty, and interest of the fabric, transforming cloth into a work of art. Dyeing is the first step in the layering process; additional layers may include overdyeing with or without resists, using textile paints to add color, discharging to remove color, and printing and patterning with stamps, stencils, screens, or brushes. Metallic foils and leafs can be added as a final layer. All of these techniques are discussed in detail in subsequent chapters. This chapter provides an overview of design considerations and artistic process to guide you as you begin to combine techniques.

Immersion Dyeing as First Layer :: Overdyeing :: Tools: The *How* of Building Layers
Wet Media: The *What* of Building Layers :: Metallic Foil and Leafing as a Final Layer
Arranging Design Elements :: The Stage Play as Design Analogy

Meditation No. 1, Jane Dunnewold, 2009. Silk broadcloth with fiber-reactive dyes, flour-paste resist, screenprinting. Screenprinted text, inspired by *Sacred Contacts* by Caroline Myss: *Live in present time, Seek only the truth, Surrender your will to God, Love is the only true power, Honor thyself, Honor One another, All is One.*

IMMERSION DYEING AS FIRST LAYER

As the first step in the layering process, dyes set the stage for all of the layers to come. Experiment with color and with manipulating the fabric. Consider overdyeing two or even three times. Explore the potential of the dyes to lay the groundwork for your own stunning fabric.

When I plan a dye session, intending to see it through to eventual layered works of art cloth, I always dye more than one piece at a time. It's efficient, because I'm not mixing chemicals and setting up a dyebath for a single piece of cloth. It's also a great way to learn to work in a series, because you can try different combinations of dye pattern, imagery, and color. If you'd like to work this way, start with at least three pieces of fabric, preferably the same fiber content and type. One-yard (91.5 cm) lengths are good; they're big enough to see the layering develop but small enough to be manageable.

the first dyebath

You'll find techniques and detailed instructions for manipulating fabric with bound-resist methods and for immersion dyeing in Chapter 3. For experienced dyers, or as an easy reference, here is a brief overview of the process for the first dyebath.

1 Pre-wash all fabric in the washing machine using hot water. Use an additive-free detergent or ½ cup (118 ml) of soda ash. Pre-washing is called *scouring* and removes oils, finishes, and dirt from fabric prior to dyeing. Dry the fabric in the dryer or hang to dry.

2 If desired, manipulate the dry fabric pieces according to the suggestions on pages 48–51. Make sure the manipulations (rubber banding, tying, compacting, etc.) are tight, so they'll resist as intended.

3 Mix the chemical water as indicated in the directions for immersion dyeing on page 46.

4 Immerse fabrics in dyebaths.

5 Batch and process according to the directions on page 47.

6 Dry the fabric, iron it, and hang it up to evaluate the results of the first dyebath. As the layers develop, it's best to hang the cloth so you can view it from a distance. Try a pin-up board, clothesline, or piece of foam core leaning against the wall.

Manipulated fabric in the dyebath.

OVERDYEING

Preparing fabric for immersion in a second dye-bath is a surefire way to add visual complexity to cloth. A single immersion dyebath provides color variation, but unless a mixed dye color splits during the batching time, most fabric immersed in a dyebath emerges as one color. Overdyeing fabric introduces a new color to the surface and contributes additional patterning if the fabric is also manipulated prior to the second dyeing. Here are some basic ideas about what to do after the initial dyebath.

manipulated pattern

Consider two approaches when determining the manipulation best suited to the fabric and your goal.

First, there is the *theme-and-variation* strategy, where you follow the lead of what you've already created and do it again, building relationship by introducing a second version of the original patterning. In other words, if the fabric was pleated the first time, pleat it again a second time. Try offsetting the pleats slightly or pleat against the pattern already created to generate visual interest. If rings were rubber-banded for the first dyebath, then tie rings again. Offset the rings so they overlap with the previously generated ones. Don't put rings right on top of previous rings. Spreading them out makes the surface more interesting.

Overdyed cloth.

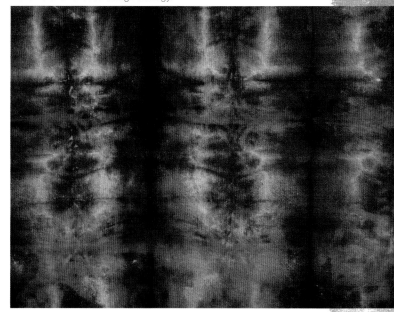

A theme-and-variation design strategy.

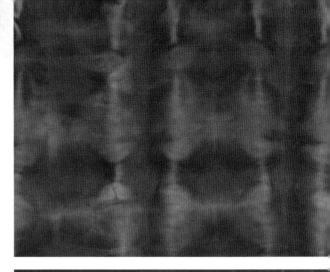

The second approach is to choose a method of manipulation that provides *contrast*. Pick a different manipulation from the one selected the first time. For example, if fabric was pleated for the first dyebath, use rubber bands to make rings for the second dyebath. The new patterning will read as circles against the straight lines of the pleating. If a triangle fold was used for the first dyebath, try rings located at the intersections of the triangle patterning for contrast.

Both methods—building relationship with theme and variation and creating contrast—are effective. Don't worry too much at this stage about patterning; just have some fun and experiment.

color choice

In addition to selecting the manipulation for fabric prior to overdyeing, give some thought to the color of the second immersion bath. As with the manipulations, there are two considerations for color choice.

The first choice is a safe choice: analogous colors, neighboring on the color wheel and in relationship with each other. Because they already have something in common, analogous colors work together when combined. For example, dye red in orange or purple, the two colors on either side of it on a basic color wheel. Dye blue in green or purple, the two colors on either side of blue on the color wheel.

Some color wheels feature more colors than the six primary and secondary colors. Studying a detailed wheel clearly demonstrates the complex color combinations possible when overdyeing fabric. If you don't have color theory background, or this is new information, purchase a color wheel to use as a reference when making color decisions for overdyeing.

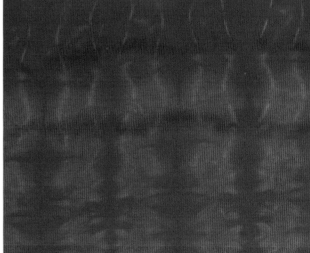

High-contrast (top) and analogous color combinations (bottom).

The second choice, high-contrast color combinations, generates a different kind of visual interest. To experiment with high-contrast color combinations, overdye by going directly across the color wheel to the complement of the color already on the fabric. For example, if the fabric is yellow, overdye it in purple. If the fabric is blue, then orange or rust generates striking contrast.

To ensure that overdyeing doesn't make "mud," it's important to make the manipulations tight. Otherwise, dye will flow into the resisted areas and alter the color, sometimes to the detriment of the design process.

Overdyeing fabric is usually successful if color choices are based on relationships that already exist between the colors on the color wheel. Selecting a color that doesn't have a clear relationship to the existing color on the fabric can create a jarring, discordant color combination. Use the color wheel as a guide and stick to the above combinations while you are developing a personal palette.

saturation

Understanding *saturation* is another key to successful overdyeing. In the context of dyeing, *saturation* means whether or not there is still space available for dye on a fiber molecule, after the first dyebath is completed. Every fiber type has a finite number of spaces on the fiber molecule where dye can attach. Several factors affect whether or not fiber molecules will "fill up" with dye molecules in a dyebath. They include:

❖ *Whether the fabric was manipulated.* If it was, there is probably light or even white space available where the fabric was tightly bound. This is open space for dye the second time around.

❖ *The strength of the dyebath.* There has to be enough dye in the dyebath to provide dye molecules for every available fiber molecule. Too few dye molecules means leftover space for additional molecules when the dyebath is completed.

❖ *The amount of cloth immersed in the dyebath.* The more fabric there is in the bucket, the more dye it will take to completely saturate the fabric and eliminate the ability to dye the cloth again.

If fabric is dyed in a strong dyebath without any manipulation, there is a good chance that saturation will occur—the available fiber molecules will react completely with dye molecules—and overdyeing won't be possible. Fabric could be dyed a brilliant golden yellow, and later immersed in a purple dyebath. If saturation occurred in the first dyebath, the fabric will still be bright yellow after the second washout. There wasn't anywhere for the purple dye to bond, so it all washed out in the last rinse.

When overdyeing, keep these cautions in mind:

❖ Lightweight silk saturates quickly, so there isn't much space for additional color after the first dyebath.

❖ Silk charmeuse wicks like crazy, so it is hard to keep any white space at all unless the fabric is manipulated very tightly. Put two pieces of fabric together and treat them as one for better results.

❖ The more layers of dye added through successive baths, the fewer available fabric molecules there are, until a new color won't react at all.

To achieve texture and fractured patterning, experimentation and note keeping are valuable. Limit variables by dyeing one fabric for an extended period of time. When you can predict saturation accurately on that cloth most of the time, begin to experiment with a new fabric type.

the second dyebath

After you've dyed and dried a piece of fabric and hung it where it can be studied, evaluate it. Does the color please you, and did it turn out the way you envisioned? Is it a deep enough color, too pale, or too deep? Did the manipulation develop the patterning you anticipated?

Make decisions for each of the pieces you've dyed. What color will each piece be dyed next? What manipulation will you choose? If each of the first three pieces was manipulated identically the first time, select a different manipulation for each of them now. This adds interest to the series and builds your experience base.

Write down your plans for the second round of dyebaths, so you'll remember what you decided to do! Then proceed with dyeing, following the instructions for immersion dyeing on page 46.

the third dyebath

Sometimes two dyebaths aren't sufficient. The selected color combination didn't work as you imagined it would, or unexpected color asserted itself through striking and separation. The patterning is wonky. What to do?

The only thing stopping a third (or fourth) dyebath from being a possibility is the question of saturation and your goals. If the fabric being dyed needs to sell for a certain price, then a third dyebath may waste time and limit your return on the investment. However, if a third dyebath could resolve the color or design problem, it's worth trying. When the fabric doesn't change much from the second dyebath to the third, it's an indication the fiber molecules are fully reacted, and saturation has been achieved. When that happens, resolve the color or design problem with textile paint, discharging, or a combination of both.

Art cloth made with multiple dyebaths.

TOOLS FOR CREATING LAYERS

After dyeing and overdyeing, build the next layers with print and pattern by using tools—the *how*— to apply wet media—the *what*. You'll have several choices of wet media to add or subtract color—textile paints, dye paste, resists, or discharge methods—and several choices of tools that you can use to make marks with wet media. First we'll look at tools, the *how* of mark-making: stamping, stenciling, silkscreening, or hand-painting.

Stenciled triangles add interest.

stamps

Stamps may be small in stature, but they are the foundation of layering imagery on cloth. Use stamps to generate an overall background pattern or use clusters of stamps to generate larger focal points. Stamp with a discharging agent, stabilize the fabric, and then reintroduce the stamped element in textile paint. If you love the look of stamps but want to print a large area faster than 2" (5 cm) stamps permit, turn stamp designs into a Thermofax, stencil, or silkscreen. Allow stamps to inspire a set of larger stencil or screen images that can be combined with the smaller tool to produce effective layers of color and pattern. The inexpensive cost of the materials is freeing. Got ideas? Get going!

stencils

Develop an entire piece of art cloth by using one or more stencils in a variety of applications. First, discharge with the stencil to introduce a lighter color, contrasting design element, and then print the image a second or third time with paint or thickened dye. Try offsetting some of the printed paint elements over the discharged layer. This interplay develops shadow elements and builds immediate relationship since the same shape is repeated in more than one form. Finishing the piece with adhesive applied through the stencil and a pleasing metallic leaf adds visual flourish. An entire series might be developed around this basic strategy. How can anyone ever be bored?

screenprinting with silkscreens or thermofax screens

There are more than a dozen ways to use screen-printing as a printing tool, but in every case, wet media is pulled across the surface of taut fabric stretched on a frame, and printing occurs on the base fabric. Silkscreens feature industry-grade polyester mesh secured to a wooden or alumi-num frame, but other frames can be adapted for printing, and polyester window sheer is an inex-pensive alternative to pricier commercial mesh. Thermofaxes are small, specialized versions of a silkscreen. Screenprinting deposits a very sheer, even layer of wet medium onto the base fabric. The fact that multiple images are printed many times from one screen makes the screen a worthwhile investment.

handpainting

Handpainting or drawing is the fourth means of embellishing fabric. Brushstrokes range from fluid to short, staccato marks. A permanent marker produces a thick or thin line, depending on the tip width. Handpainting suits applications of dye, discharge medium, and paint or foil adhesive, but in every case, the maker's hand is the force behind the mark, and the effect is very different from the three other methods described above.

You may wonder whether it matters if you are proficient at creating and handling all four of the methods I've just described. The answer is simple: yes. Each tool has a characteristic ap-pearance, which can be used to your advantage if you know what those characteristics are. It's also helpful to understand the strengths and limitations of each tool, so you can choose just the right tool for the job. Nothing is more frus-trating than stamping on a heavy, loosely woven fabric only to have the image disintegrate before your eyes. It's not about you! Stamping works best on smooth fabric. Choose stenciling or handpainting for the loose weaves, and you will have paired the right tool with the right fabric—the ultimate goal if mark-making is to succeed every time.

These samples incorporate handprinted soy-wax elements with handpainting.

WET MEDIA: THE *WHAT* OF BUILDING LAYERS

Art cloth by Marcia Murphy.

What to apply with the tools you create? You have several choices of wet media that will add or remove color or act as a resist to restrain color. When it comes to adding color, I recommend that you begin learning to make layered art cloth with pieces that combine immersion dyeing with textile paints, applied with stamps, stencils, screens, or brushes, before moving on to printing with dye paste.

water-soluble resists

Water-soluble resists, which block a portion of the fabric from accepting color or discharge and then wash out of the fabric, can accommodate a variety of layering strategies. Just a few of the possibilities:

- applying resist to white fabric before an immersion dyebath;
- applying resist to white fabric before a layer of printing with dye;
- applying resist to dyed fabric prior to overdyeing;
- applying resist to dyed fabric prior to discharging;
- applying resist to a fabric that has already been dyed, resisted, and dyed again (you can alternate multiple applications of dyeing and resisting numerous times);
- applying resist to white or colored fabric prior to handpainting or printing with thinned textile paint.

Maybe you've already decided what sort of resist to apply to your fabric in progress. If you're completing more than one piece as part of a sampling exercise, there are numerous options. Write a strategy before beginning. Try these processes, remembering to follow the instructions for stabilizing every process added to the cloth before a new layer is added.

1 Configure fabric and dip sides or corners in hot soy wax. Overdye in an immersion dyebath.

2 Apply wax with a brush or roller, using a textured surface underneath the fabric. Overdye in an immersion dyebath.

3 Stencil hot wax onto the cloth. Handpaint with thickened dye.

4 Apply wax to the folded corners of the fabric and discharge the cloth in a thiourea dioxide (thiox) or Rit Color Remover bath.

Cloth patterned with resists.

5 Squeegee flour paste over the entire fabric surface. Crackle when dry and paint with thinned black paint.

6 Stencil water-soluble glue onto the fabric. Allow it to dry. Handpaint dye across the surface.

7 Stencil or screen water-soluble glue onto cotton fabric and allow it to dry. Apply a thickened chlorine bleach product to the surface with a foam brush. Wash immediately.

8 Selectively apply flour paste to areas of the cloth—as solid circles, for example. When the flour paste dries, crackle it and then use a brush to paint over the paste with thinned paint. When the flour is removed the areas where the circles were added will feature the fine lines and cracks that are the hallmark of the process.

discharging

Discharging is the removal of color from fabric. Plan discharged elements early in the layering process, before paint, foil, or metallic leaf is added. Discharging is appropriate when dyeing is completed, but it's also appropriate prior to the final overdye of the fabric or as a series of alternating steps back and forth between dyeing and discharging.

Select dye and discharge applications based on the colors achieved by discharging. If the discharged color is compatible with the original dye color, another dyebath is not necessarily required. If discharged color is at odds with the original dye color, another dyebath is a good idea. Complete discharging prior to applications of textile paint, foil, or leafing, because then there isn't any chance that surface sheen or texture will be compromised.

Choose discharge agents based on the selected fabric type—protein (silk, wool) or cellulose (cotton, rayon, hemp, or linen). All agents are compatible with cellulose, but bleach products cannot be used on protein fibers. Dyed silk can be discharged in a thiox bath, with Rit Color Remover, by printing thickened thiox paste or by printing with Jacquard Discharge Paste. All of these treatments, as well as chlorine bleach products, can be used on cotton, rayon, or linen dyed fabric.

Choose a discharge application for the fabric in progress. Stabilize and then determine if the cloth requires a new dyebath to integrate the original dyed color with the discharged color or if the two are compatible. It's possible to dye and discharge fabric several times, generating subtle patterning and color shifting in the process. Play with variations on this theme and arrive at several satisfactory selections for your repertoire.

Art cloth with discharged elements.

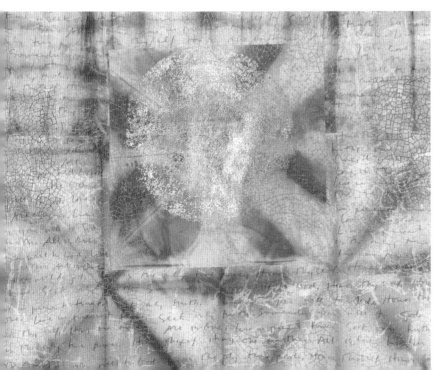

Discharging adds interest by removing color.

METALLIC FOIL AND LEAF AS FINAL LAYER

Cloth with metallic treatment as final layer.

Metallic foil or leaf is not necessary for every piece of art cloth, but when these additions are appropriate to the design and well integrated, they add beauty, richness, and elegance. Add these treatments at the end of the layering process. Choose from these ideas:

❖ Select a design element that was printed in paint. Add it in foil or leaf. Choose the color based on the color scheme. Is it predominantly cool? Silver or copper foil will look great. Is the color scheme a warm range of rust, orange, or red? Gold will shimmer beautifully against those colors. Always print fewer of the foil or leaf accents than were printed in paint. This element is meant to move the viewer's eyes across the fabric. Printing too many foil or leaf images makes a surface static. Position the shiny accents so that they guide the eye across the cloth.

❖ Add a new accent to the fabric, introducing not only textural contrast (shiny leaf versus matte cloth) but also shape contrast. If a series of rectangles was discharged and printed in paint, add contrasting foil circles or triangles. If flowers are the dominant theme, add metal leaf leaves as the accent.

❖ Add organic fusible shapes to the fabric. Gently pull the fusible web apart into loose organic shapes or cut it into thin strips and then stretch the strips gently to warp them. The webby appearance of the fusible translates into equally webby metallic accents.

❖ Add a smaller version of a pre-existing design element in silver foil or leaf. Hand tint the element with textile paint, integrating it into the surface by matching it to paint used for earlier printing.

Leafing may or may not complete the piece of art cloth you have produced. While this book can't possibly cover the possibilities for stitching, embroidery, paper lamination, or additional enhancements, there are resources available to guide the work, should you feel something more is needed to complete the piece. I encourage you to explore techniques you may have perfected outside the realm of wet-process surface design. It's the commingling of wet and dry processes, old and new, contrast and relationship, that make each artist's work unique. Don't be afraid to try something you may never have considered before reading this book. Discovering what can happen is worth the risk.

ARRANGING DESIGN ELEMENTS

If you created a busy background texture with dyeing and/or discharging, keep the elements you print with paint simple. If the dyed/discharged background is quiet, simple, or subtle, make printed elements more complex. There are two ways to add elements:

1 Choose a tool (stamp, stencil, screen, or some other device you've acquired) to register printed images across the entire surface. If using stamps, print the stamps side by side all over the fabric. Try combining a series of stamps to fill space and cover the surface. This approach to printing adds interest to a dully dyed fabric and knocks out unappealing color from the dye.

2 Scatter imagery across the fabric as though tossing elements down onto the cloth. Think of the surface as having a net cast across it. The intersections in the netting indicate placement for printing. Try folding the fabric and iron in the creases temporarily to mimic a grid. The goal is to learn to print by trusting your eye to determine placement and balance. Remember the concept of "tossing" the images down onto the cloth and resist

Sometimes a busy background benefits from the addition of a simple element such as a solid circle, added here in metallic gold paint.

the impulse to line up the elements in a regular pattern. Try printing images on clear transparencies so you can lay an image on the fabric and audition its placement.

After the first printed elements dry, try adding a second set of painted or printed elements. Choose a scattered orientation for these elements, too. Add printed elements until the surface is visually full. Beginners often fear going overboard.

Avoid clumping printed elements together. Make sure elements are evenly spaced and also beginning to overlap slightly. Not all images will overlap this time around, but at least a few of this round of printing should overlap the first ones, as overlapping is the key to implying depth. The message the brain gets is, "if elements are overlapped, one must be in front and one must be in back." This, along with ordering size by introducing small, medium, and large images, and incorporating value from light to dark or vice-versa, creates depth on the surface of the cloth.

Scattered imagery creates dynamic movement.

THE STAGE PLAY AS DESIGN ANALOGY

Repeating visual elements provide unity or continuity to a design.

I think it's useful to see your design process as a stage play. Some productions have huge casts; others feature two leading players in dialogue with each other. But no matter what form a play takes, every actor is needed. Even the smallest role helps move the play forward to a successful conclusion. Here are the parts of the "visual play" you must consider as you build your own production:

background

Perhaps you want to create a crowd scene with lots of bodies. Perhaps there aren't any speaking roles, but the street scene wouldn't ring true if the crowd were absent. Visual examples:

* Tone-on-tone, printed representational patterning.

* Tone-on-tone, printed nonrepresentational patterning.

* Texture: either tone-on-tone or contrasting.

* Nonspecific patterning generated by dyeing the fabric with manipulation.

* Textural additions: stitching, beading, etc.

Or perhaps you envision a scene that is not a crowd but still includes nonspeaking, individual background roles: separate actors who pass through a scene without having a speaking role. An example would be people walking down a street or diners in a restaurant scene who aren't engaged in dialogue. Visual examples:

* Any of the above examples, but used in fewer numbers, so the background feels more spacious.

supporting cast

These are speaking roles that contribute important information to the development of the plot, but they are not the leading actors. Visual examples:

* Design elements that contrast with the background. Contrast comes from differences in size, shape, color, value, texture, style, and/or theme. For example, a design element based on a tiny element printed as background may be reintroduced as a medium-size element in a new color.

* In the context of a pieced quilt, the small designs on the fabric could be considered the crowd scene and the medium-size pieces that fit together could be called the supporting cast.

* Design elements that build relationship, contribute repetition, or help integrate the surface are also supporting cast members. The same qualities that generate contrast are used to build relationship—size, shape, color, value, texture, style, and/or theme.

leading roles

These are the stars of the production. The story revolves around them. There may be one leading actor or actress or several. An ensemble production is a slightly different take on the leading role scenario. Visual examples:

❖ Leading actors on the visual stage: a high-contrast element used alone or as a series of focal points that guide the eye across the surface. Shiny texture, size, the use of a complementary color.

❖ Ensemble acting: crystallographic distribution of elements.

❖ One leading role, with a soliloquy or monologue: a mandala or single centrally located motif.

❖ A dialogue or duet: two well-balanced focal-point motifs.

❖ An evenly distributed conversation: three or more elements that lead the eye, often setting up a triangular series of focal points.

showtime!

To improve your work, study your *cast* of design elements and colors. Make sure every single one contributes to your visual production. A rogue cameo appearance, an actor who stumbles over her lines, or actors who are ambiguous in their roles are examples of parts that should have been eliminated or changed, to keep the story moving smoothly. We've all watched a film with an actor whose role wasn't clear, where we found ourselves questioning his or her presence—why was s/he there? What did s/he have to do with the other events happening on the screen? Be a firm *director* and don't cast any element you can't explain or justify. If in doubt, talk it out.

In overall patterning, the parts work together to support a strong visual element.

adding color:
fiber-reactive dyes and textile paints

Dyes and textile paints add color to fabric. Dyeing fabric is an important part of producing a complex layered surface, and in this book, we'll explore fiber-reactive dyes. Reliable, easy to find, economical, and safe, fiber-reactive dyes are a good choice for beginners but are also beloved by experienced dyers, who often pair them with other dyes to achieve specialized effects. Fiber-reactive dyes are extremely versatile; whether the goal is a series of evenly dyed values for a quilt, a brightly colored T-shirt, or a complex layered print pattern, the dyes can do it. Textile paints are another way to add vibrant color to cloth and are available in a vast range of hues and effects.

Fiber-reactive Dyes :: Dye Processes :: The Immersion Method :: Manipulating Fabric Prior to Dyeing
Printing on Fabric with Dyes :: Textile Paints :: Color and Textile Paints :: Troubleshooting

Detail, Dichotomy No. 1: Two Sides to Every Story, Jane Dunnewold, 2009.
Silk noil with fiber-reactive dyes, thiox discharge, and metal leaf applied
with screened adhesive.

UNDERSTANDING FIBER-REACTIVE DYES

The dyeing process isn't complicated; there are as many approaches to using fiber-reactive dyes as there are people teaching and dyeing with them. Students sometimes comment that studying the chemistry of dyes is intimidating, but an understanding of how dyes work allows you to choose among a wide variety of options, increases your control over the process, and protects you. Using chemicals of any kind introduces intrinsic hazards, and understanding potential hazards ensures both your safety and that of those around you.

Fiber-reactive dyes are manufactured in several different formulations. In this book, we use the fiber-reactive MX series of dyes, also referred to as Procion dyes (Procion is the original name on the now-expired patent). Today, the term *Procion* is used interchangeably with the term *fiber-reactive MX dye*. Numerous companies sell MX dyes. These dyes are all synthetic and suitable for use on any natural fiber—silk, rayon, cotton, linen, and wool. Large manufacturers produce pure, unmixed dye colors. Smaller companies buy the pure colors from the manufacturer and then use those dyes to mix their own proprietary colors.

Fiber-reactive dyes are appealing for their color and lightfast quality. The dye molecules react chemically with the fiber molecules and unite through electron sharing, called a covalent bond; the two molecules, fiber and dye, become one. This contributes to the dye's permanency. Unattached dye molecules wash away in the rinse water.

One beauty of working with dyes is that the bond occurring between molecules doesn't change the hand, feel, or drape of the fabric. Other surface design applications alter the hand of the cloth, and sometimes that's not consistent with the goal an artist has in mind.

Dyeing fabric successfully requires a controlled environment related to three conditions of the process: time, temperature, and dyebath chemicals. Your goals for dyeing will determine the best conditions for the results you seek. For evenly dyed fabric (referred to as *level dyeing*), I'd set up the dyebath quite differently from a dyebath intended to generate texture or crystal-like patterning.

Dyeing with fiber-reactive MX dyes is an easy process to begin in one simple dye session. But as you'll see, there are endless variations and subtleties inherent in the process. By limiting variables at the beginning—using the same fabric for an extended period of time, measuring accurately, always using water from the same source, etc.—you can achieve satisfying and repeatable results. You'll know why you got what you got, and also how to do it again. It's worth making a few basic notes to support future dye projects (see Creating a Dye Notebook, page 40).

methods of working with dye

In this book, our goal is to produce textured, variably colored patterning, as the perfect background for additional printed layering. This is accomplished with one of two methods: immersion dyeing or printing with thickened dye. This chapter provides instructions for both methods.

Immersion dyeing involves submerging cloth in a dyebath of dye and chemical water solution for a period of time, during which the dye and fiber molecules react. Once the fabric is removed from the dye and rinsed, the color is permanent. Printing with dye requires a different set of auxiliary chemicals than those used in an immersion dyebath. Immersion dyeing and printed dye can be combined to produce wonderful results. As you're learning, concentrate on one process first. After you've developed confidence mixing immersion dyebaths, add the printing component to your repertoire.

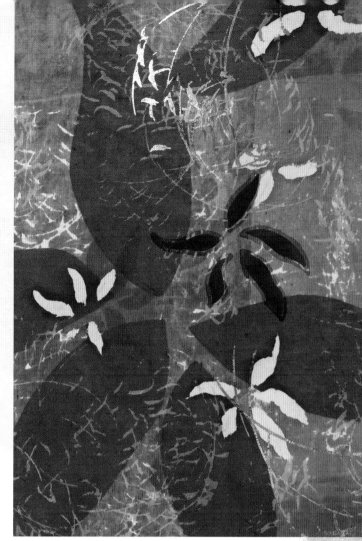

Apparent Wisdom by Lisa Kerpoe shows the possibilities of printing with dye.

Immersion dyeing produces a range of gorgeous colors and patterns.

COMPONENTS FOR DYE PROCESSES

Dyeing requires fabric, dye color, water, and auxiliary chemicals, as well as the knowledge and skill of the dyer in evaluating and combining components. While nothing takes the place of practice and experience, the following descriptions of components for dye processes will prepare you for successful dyeing.

fabric

Fiber-reactive dyes react only with natural fibers, including cotton, silk, wool, rayon, and linen. They do not react with synthetic fibers. Specialty dye houses sell fabric labeled as PFD, or Prepared for Dyeing. PFD fabrics are not treated with any finish that can inhibit the dye reaction. Many commercial fabrics, especially fabrics intended for quilting, are treated with finishes designed to be lightfast, colorfast, or wrinkle resistant. That's all well and good for a quiltmaker, but it makes a dyer's life miserable! Yet even PFD fabrics have a light finish for visual appeal in the marketplace, so any fabric, including those labeled PFD, should be washed prior to being dyed.

There are several factors in the relationship between fabric and dye that influence the final outcome. Natural fabrics come in a wide array of weights and styles; these qualities influence the dye process, and will affect the amount of dye used in the dyebath. A heavier weight and weave of cloth requires more dye powder than would a lighter fabric of the same type to dye the same approximate color value. In other words, if I want to dye sheer cotton voile and cotton broadcloth the same depth of color, it will take less dye to color the voile and more dye to color the broadcloth. Though both are cotton fabrics, the relative weight of the fabrics affects how much dye is needed.

Dye molecules also bond to fiber molecules of different fabric types at different rates of speed. The bonding action is called *striking*. Dye molecules strike at different rates related to their relative size. Red dye strikes faster on silk fabric than other colors, for example. Blue dye is slower to strike or react on any fabric. All dyes react more slowly on cotton and rayon than they do on silk.

The amount of fabric in the dyebath also affects the depth of color on the finished cloth. The quantity of dye in a dyebath, including a low-water immersion dyebath, is finite. It makes sense that 2 yards or meters of fabric dyed in the bath will yield a deeper color than 4 yards or meters of fabric in a similar dyebath. The dye distributes across the yardage, and the same amount of color is being spread over more volume of cloth.

dye color

Let's talk for a moment about the gorgeous dye colors available from dye suppliers. The Colour Index, an international manufacturer's directory for pigments and dyes, lists twenty-four pure MX colors. About half of these are not currently in production, probably due to environmental toxicity issues. In the United States, eleven or twelve pure dye colors are available to the home studio dyer. Since these colors are pure, the weight and weave of the fabric may affect how the color looks, but it will be the same color on silk that it is on cotton or rayon.

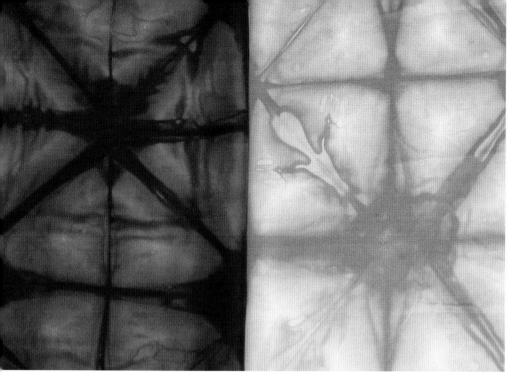

Mixed colors strike at different rates and can create surprising combinations of color.

Mixed colors are proprietary recipes and vary from company to company, even though all mixed colors are combinations of the same pure colors. It's easy to be seduced by the color names given by the manufacturing company. However, we all see color differently, and Chinese Red to me may not be Chinese Red to you. Adding that different dye colors within a single color formula have the potential to *strike at different rates* on different fabrics, and the use of mixed color is a challenge! More than one dyer has been mystified by the appearance of red on a piece of silk broadcloth when she thought she was dyeing violet.

For example, with a mixed purple dye, the red dye molecules may strike faster than the blue dye molecules, separating during the dyebath, and generating terrific violet/red patterning, but not what was intended! This might be considered gorgeous serendipity, but it could also be considered a disaster. Knowing that it may happen will help to temper disappointment or surprise at the results of the dyebath.

Pure colors stay true on all fabrics and are intermixable.

auxiliary chemicals for immersion dyeing

Because there are so many approaches to dyeing with fiber-reactive MX dyes, it's helpful to classify the additional chemicals (called *auxiliary* chemicals) used during dyeing as either *negotiable* or *non-negotiable*. Negotiable chemicals are those required for one dyeing process, but not necessarily every dyeing process, such as salt. Non-negotiable components are essential, no matter which dye application you're utilizing.

non-negotiable components for dyeing

Non-negotiable components are essential to dyeing in any application.

Dye Dye amounts vary per dyebath. Experienced dyers refer to the amount of dye needed as *to taste*. That isn't a culinary term; rather it references personal preference. Dyers who prefer rich, deep color use more dye than those who prefer pale colors. You can determine exactly how much dye to use by weighing the fabric and adding dye according to industry standards; dye websites provide this information free of charge. If your goal is textured dyed surfaces, you can learn to eyeball the amount of dye needed to get the final color you seek.

Soda ash Soda ash (sodium carbonate) is an alkali that *fixes* the dye, locking the molecules in place so that they become one with the fiber molecules. If soda ash is left out of the formula, the color will not be permanent. Some color may remain due to staining, but it fades in later washes.

Temperature Dyes react best between 70 and 100°F (21.1 to 37.7°C), so the dye solution should be within that range when the dyebath is prepared. Water that feels warm on your wrist is within the acceptable temperature range. If the water temperature is too hot, dye begins to bond immediately with the water and less dye is available for the fabric. On the other hand, cold water slows the ability of the dye molecules to move and react, so fabric may look bright prior to washing but pale afterward because the dye molecules didn't fully react with the cloth.

Water Water dissolves the dye in dyebath or a printed application. Water hardness, or mineral content, compromises the quality of dyed color. Adding water softener or using distilled bottled water improves reactivity and affects color in areas of the world where water is hard.

negotiable components for dyeing

The following chemicals are negotiable components of dye usage (required in one or more dyeing processes, but not every dyeing process) with a brief description of their purpose and appropriate application.

Calsolene oil Calsolene oil is an ingredient added to dyebaths for level dyeing; it encourages dye to react uniformly across the cloth's surface.

Ludigol Ludigol is a brand name for sodium m-nitrobenzene sulfonic acid, a brightener sometimes added to a dyebath to support the intensity of color.

Metaphos A water softener, metaphos (sodium hexametaphosphate) helps dye dissolve uniformly and helps keep dye particles in suspension. Low-water immersion dyebaths don't always require water softener, and the patterns created by minerals in hard water can be interesting. Calgon is a substitute for metaphos.

Salt Salt is included in traditional dyebaths because it effectively forces dye molecules out of suspension in water and into the fabric, where bonding to the fiber molecules occurs. Traditional dyebaths used more water than today's

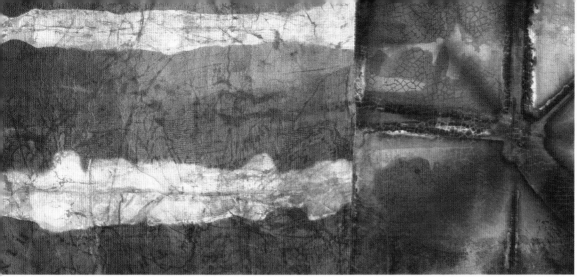

Immersion dyeing is the first step in building layers.

low-water applications, and the salt was important because the fabric floated in a bath of dye solution. Dye molecules had to be encouraged to leave the water and penetrate the cloth, and the salt served this purpose. In low-water dyebaths, the water is almost entirely absorbed by the cloth, so you might think that salt isn't necessary in this setting, as I did. But after several months of trials, the fabrics dyed in baths that included salt were definitely brighter than those dyed without it, so I put salt back into my dye equation.

Sodium alginate A seaweed-based thickener for dyes, sodium alginate is never used in a low-water immersion application; it's reserved for printing and handpainting applications.

Synthrapol Synthrapol is a brand of mild detergent formulated to remove migrant (unattached) dye molecules from fabric during the wash. Synthrapol acts as a surfactant (shorthand for *SURFace ACTive AgeNT*), affecting surface tension to ease migrant dye into the rinse water and out of the cloth. A small amount of Synthrapol also helps dye dissolve completely in preparation for printing.

Urea Urea is an ingredient that functions as a *humectant* (a substance that retains moisture), keeping moisture from evaporating quickly so that dye molecules have more time to react

with fiber molecules. Urea is usually included in a dye-printing recipe because the exposed printed surface needs as much damp reaction time as possible, but is almost never used in a low-water immersion bath.

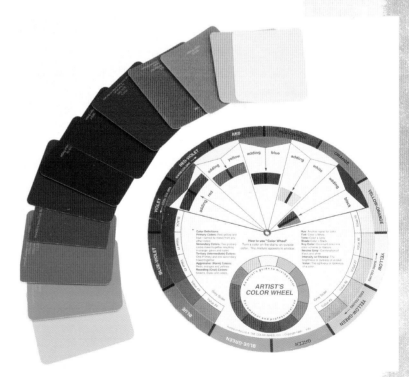

See page 170 for instructions on dyeing a color wheel.

A dye notebook helps you to organize information about MX dyes for quick reference. Keeping a complete notebook in your studio allows you to check dye color on various fabrics and also provides advance information concerning the colors *hidden* in a dye recipe. *Hidden colors* are those in the formula you don't automatically see or know are there. For example, red dye is included in an olive dye formula. It shifts the green color from the pure color wheel green to the dirtier version we call olive. Completing the exercise of creating a dye notebook gives you immediate access to color information you can't retrieve any other way. It only takes one studio session, and it will be an invaluable resource.

SUPPLIES

- MX dyes on hand in the studio (or whatever you've purchased if you are starting from scratch)
- 1 yard (91.5 cm) of cotton sheeting or muslin
- 1 yard (91.5 cm) of 12mm silk habotai (China silk)
- 1 yard (91.5 cm) of rayon/viscose challis

Note: You can add other fabrics, such as silk noil, linen, hemp, or other cotton fabrics.

- Soda ash
- 1-cup (237 ml) containers, one for each dye color you have (plastic ziplock bags or yogurt containers are fine)
- Salt
- Plastic spoons, one for each dye color
- Dust mask
- Rubber gloves
- Spray bottle with fine mist setting
- Loose-leaf notebook
- Paper to mount the notebook samples
- Glue stick
- Permanent marker (or computer) to label samples and pages
- Steam iron
- Scissors or rotary cutter and cutting mat
- Three-ring hole punch or the binding services of a copy shop

A dye notebook is an invaluable companion as your dyeing repertoire expands.

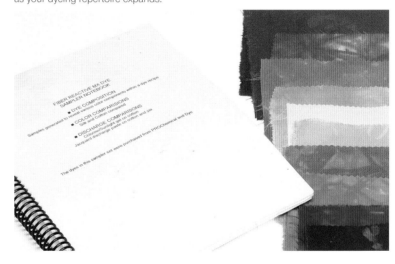

Assemble the supplies before you begin working on your notebook.

part one:

testing for hidden colors in MX dyes

These samples reveal the hidden colors in a dye formula. All fiber-reactive MX dyes are either pure colors (I call them *parents* because the rest of the colors are made from them) or a color mixed from several other colors. Maybe it seems obvious, but not knowing a color is a mixed color skews your whole color plan. If you don't realize in advance that the wonderful navy you just purchased has red in it, you may be in for quite a surprise.

1 Cut 2" (5 cm) squares of cotton broadcloth for every dye color intended for testing.

2 Lay the squares in a row, on a table covered with a sheet or other absorbent padding. Don't use plastic; a nonabsorbent table surface contributes to bleeding or wicking if the fabric gets too wet.

3 Lightly dampen the fabric by misting it lightly with water. Don't overdo it.

4 Wearing a mask and gloves, dip the end of a plastic spoon into a container of dye, picking up a few particles of dye on the tip of the spoon.

5 Tap the spoon against the first square of cotton. Grains of dye should knock off onto the fabric square.

6 If you misted lightly, the dampness of the fabric will encourage the dye powder to dissolve just a bit, revealing individual colors hidden in the formula.

7 Allow the samples to dry. They do not need to be washed or set. They are only samples and will never be washed in the future.

8 When the samples are dry, press each square. Mount the squares on copy paper with the glue stick. Print the name of the dye, the product number, and the company/producer on the copy paper before gluing the samples to the paper. This labeling can be done by hand, but it can also be printed on the computer.

HAVANA BROWN
5214

BLACK
602A

BLACK
608

DEEP BLACK
609

Colors hidden in a mixed dye formula separate when the dye is sprinkled on damp fabric.

Important: Keep track of the dyes so you know which colors are sprinkled on particular samples. If you have a large number of samples and you don't keep track, you'll never know which colors the swatches represent. When I made my notebook, I put the dyes in a row on the table and then placed swatches in front of them as I worked.

Organize the samples so you can keep track of the colors you're dyeing.

Mixed colors may be quite different when applied to different fabric types; these samples compare cotton and silk.

part two:

dye on different fabric types

This set of samples is a visual record of the potential variations of dye color on different fabric types. Pure colors look the same on cotton, silk, and rayon because the dye formula is just one color, so individual particles don't strike separately. Make pure color samples in addition to the mixed color samples, so you have a complete sample set. If the dye is a mixed color, the samples may look quite different from each other. A record of what mixed dye colors look like on a variety of fabrics is helpful when a new project is in the planning stage.

1 Cut 2" (5 cm) squares of the fabrics you intend to dye. In my notebook, I used silk habotai and cotton sheeting.

2 Wearing gloves and a mask, mix up the chemical solution:
   1 gallon (3.8 liters) hot water
   ⅓ cup (79 ml) soda ash
   ½ cup (118 ml) salt

Stir thoroughly as soon as the chemicals are added to the water and continue stirring until the salt and soda ash are dissolved. **Note:** Adjust the amount of water/soda/salt solution to fit the number of dyes you intend to sample.

3 Pour ½ cup (118 ml) of the solution into each of your dye containers (cup, yogurt container, or plastic bag). Stir a scant teaspoon of each dye color into the separate cups of chemical water solution. Mix thoroughly to dissolve the dye.

4 Immerse samples of each fabric in the individual dye cups. Keep your organizational system intact, so you know which colors are which! Leave the samples in the dye cups at least three hours.

5 When the time has elapsed, rinse out the samples in hot water until the water runs clear. I wash mine by hand so I can keep track of the colors.

6 Press the samples to dry them. Press with an old towel under samples as some of the color may not completely set, since the washout wasn't done by machine with detergent. For sampling, this is the easiest way to keep track of your pieces.

7 Mount the samples on paper with the glue stick. Print the name of the dye, the product number, and the company/producer on the paper. Glue the samples in cascading sets so the color similarities and differences are easy to compare.

Your health is a precious gift. Protect it. Observe practical safety measures when handling dyes as a good housekeeping practice. Fiber-reactive dyes are safe compared to other dye categories; that's one of the reasons they're popular among dyers who work in home studios. But the use of chemicals demands respect and caution. Fiber-reactive dyes are packaged in powder form, and inhaling the powder is potentially hazardous. Follow these tips for dyeing safety.

▲ Always wear a dust mask when opening and measuring dyes.

▲ Wear latex or plastic gloves to protect hands from staining.

▲ Never, under any circumstance, clean dye from your hands using chlorine bleach. The chemical reaction of dye and bleach is harder on your body than exposure to dye alone. Let the dye stain wear off your hands.

▲ Check gloves before each dye session to be sure there are no holes or leaks.

▲ Wipe up any dye solution or dry powder immediately. Wash dye-stained towels frequently. Liquid dye solution turns back into a powder when it dries. That's why it's important to clean up any spills.

▲ Once you've used containers or utensils for dyeing, never use them for food or drink.

I measure dye in the studio sink. The dye container is lower than my face, and when I measure the powder, any excess drifts down to the wet sink surface, rather than up toward my nose. I always wear a mask. The other advantage of this system is that if dye powder accidentally spills or drifts, it does so into the bottom of the sink, where I can turn on the water and wash it away. Dyes are not harmful to plumbing or pipes, so it isn't a problem to wash excess or spent dye, down the sink.

DYEING WITH THE IMMERSION METHOD

Immersion dyeing is the simplest method of dyeing, yet there are many nuances to the process. Read through the following notes on the dyeing process, which have emerged from my years of working with dyes and learning the finer points of dye and fabric behavior, before proceeding with the step-by-step instructions.

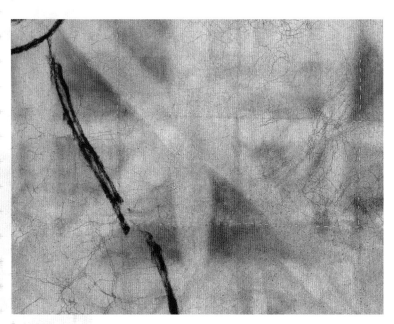

Dyeing sometimes gives unpredictable results; keep good records of recipes and dye combinations.

❖ I use a low-water method of immersion dyeing. The classic immersion dyebath requires large quantities of water and auxiliary chemicals. For example, a typical dyebath, in the conventional method, requires five gallons of water and several cups of salt to dye just a few yards of cloth. In this approach, the goal is level dyeing—smooth, even color across the yardage. Our goal is textured-looking fabric, however, so large amounts of water or salt are unnecessary. Low-water immersion dyeing is more environmentally friendly, requiring less water and smaller amounts of auxiliary chemicals; it can be done in a small bucket or even a plastic bag. As artists and human beings, we have a responsibility to the Earth, and working efficiently with its resources is an important charge.

❖ The dye-solution recipe on page 46 makes one gallon of chemical water, which is the auxiliary solution before the dye is added to it. This solution keeps indefinitely if leftovers are stored in a lidded container.

❖ Begin collecting a variety of different-sized containers to accomodate varying lengths of fabric. Yogurt-size and larger plastic containers and small baggies work well for smaller pieces. Plastic shoeboxes and small cat litter trays are great for dyeing slightly larger pieces.

❖ I add the soda ash fixer at the beginning of the dyebath. Traditional practice adds it later in the process, but because fracturing and texture are desirable in this dyeing option, it's actually beneficial to add the soda ash at the beginning. A decade of using this approach as the standard has convinced me that the early addition of the soda ash facilitates the patterning because dye molecules attach quickly and randomly. There isn't any appreciable loss of color; the fabric is vibrant and gorgeous.

❖ The amount of dye you add will be to your preference. If you're experimenting, try 1 teaspoon (5 ml) per quart of liquid (946 ml) for pale color. For deeper color, try 1 tablespoon (15 ml) of dye. Usually it's wasteful to use more than 1 tablespoon (15 ml) of dye per quart, as the fabric can only react to a finite amount of dye, and any molecules that don't attach must be washed away. Overdoing the amount of dye only extends the wash time and uses extra water. Turquoise and black are exceptions to this rule; these colors require double the amount of dye to yield the same depth of color produced by 1 tablespoon (15 ml) of other dyes.

❖ *Batching* refers to the time during which the fiber and dye molecules are reacting. Industry standards suggest that dye must be in contact with fabric for at least three hours to maximize color absorption. The fabric must also remain damp. Keeping the fabric in a container or baggie eliminates any chance of the fabric drying out, but shortening the time may affect the depth of color on your cloth, so be patient. On the other hand, the dye begins to exhaust, or break down, as soon as the soda ash is introduced, so you can't mix up dye with the chemical water and then save it for another day. **All dye must be used during the session in which it was mixed.** And since the dye is exhausting, colors won't get any deeper after about six hours; you can leave the dye overnight for convenience, but extending time to produce deeper color won't usually make much difference.

❖ Silk can be dyed in a low-water immersion bath, with confidence about the stability of the end result. The traditional approach to immersion dyeing cautions against dyeing silk fabric in a soda ash solution, because many textile artists originally dyed with reactive dyes that required steam setting. Steaming silk treated with soda ash can indeed cause damage, but the high temperature of steaming is the damaging factor, not the soda ash itself. MX dyes don't need to be steamed; batching is efficient and effective.

Silk broadcloth is lustrous and sometimes thought of as too luxurious to dye, but it dyes as easily as other fabrics and is a joy to sew.

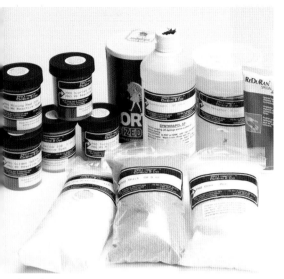

Gather the supplies needed for dyeing before you begin.

PROCESS:
LOW-WATER
IMMERSION DYEING

A low-water immersion dyebath generates a range of pale to deep color on the cloth. If the dye is a pure color, the variations are monochromatic (versions of one color). If the dye is a mixed color, the fabric may exhibit more than one color when dyeing is completed.

low-water immersion dyeing

1 Mix up the chemical solution in the bucket:
    1 gallon (3.8 liters) hot water
    ½ cup (118 ml) salt
    ⅓ cup (79 ml) soda ash

Optional:
    1 tablespoon (15 ml) metaphos or Calgon

2 Wearing the mask and gloves, add the chemicals to the water and stir immediately with your gloved hand to dissolve the chemicals. This solution will be divided into smaller containers. Leftovers can be stored indefinitely.

3 When chemicals are dissolved, scoop the water into the 1-quart (946 ml) container. Fill the container half full with solution **(fig. 1)**.

4 Add dye to the chemical water solution in the quart container **(fig. 2)**. Put the lid on securely and shake the container vigorously to dissolve the dye. Add enough chemical water to fill up the container.

5 Choose a container the appropriate size for the fabric you intend to dye. If the cloth is manipulated (folded and rubber banded, etc.), it may not take a very large container. If the cloth is loose, choose a container that will hold all of it without allowing the dye solution to overflow.

6 Pour the dye solution over the fabric; making sure the cloth is covered **(fig. 3)**. If you are using baggies, zip the bag shut and then rock it back and forth to distribute the dye solution.

SUPPLIES

- 1 yard (91.5 cm) or more of linen, cotton, silk, or rayon fabric (fabric may be manipulated according to guidelines on page 48–51 if desired)
- Dust mask
- Gloves (elbow length, available from dye suppliers)
- Bucket
- Measuring spoons
- Measuring cup
- 1-quart (946 ml) container
- Hot water
- Salt (iodized is fine)
- Soda ash
- Dye
- Extra-large ziplock plastic bags and/or additional appropriated containers, such as small buckets, large cottage cheese containers, plastic storage containers
- Synthrapol

Optional: Calgon or metaphos water softener

7 Allow the dye to batch for at least three hours and as long as overnight **(fig. 4)**.

8 When batching time has elapsed, it's time to wash out the fabric. Begin by pouring any excess dye solution into the sink.

9 Rinse the fabric briefly in cold water. Instead of running water continuously, put cold water in a bucket and stir the fabric around in the bucket.

10 If you've manipulated the fabric, untie any strings, undo rubber bands or elastics, remove Plexiglas, etc. Rinse these items separately so they can be reused.

11 Put the fabric in the washing machine, on the cool or cold setting. Choose a water level appropriate for the amount of cloth being rinsed. Add 1 teaspoon (5 ml) of Synthrapol. Set the final rinse cycle at a hot setting.

Note: Washing machines vary. Be mindful of the machine you're using to keep water usage as low as possible and to maximize the effectiveness of the wash out procedure. Consider these points:

❖ Small pieces of fabric are better washed by hand. Start with cold water and end with hot water. Be sure the water runs clear at the end of the washing/rinsing process.

❖ Most machines have numerous settings. Choose a water level that will allow the fabric to move, without excess water.

❖ A five- or six-minute rinse cycle is usually enough and saves water.

❖ Washing machines have different settings. The ideal combination is a cold cycle at the beginning and a hot cycle at the end. The hot cycle sets the dye. If your machine doesn't offer that combination, you can set each cycle manually or reverse the hoses on the back of the machine so hot and cold are swapped. Most machines have a hot/cold choice, and if the hoses are reversed, you get what you need.

❖ Dry the fabric in a dryer once the wash out is complete. Fabric may also dry on a clothesline, or you can complete the drying process by ironing.

The foundation of the layered fabric surface is the textured background produced by dyeing. Manipulating the fabric prior to immersing it in a dyebath generates pattern and texture. Pleating, folding, and scrunching are just a few of the manipulations classified as *bound resists*, which says it all. The goal of each manipulation is to isolate sections of fabric so dye can't penetrate the cloth. (Other kinds of resists, which are used after the initial dyebaths to add print and pattern to the cloth, are discussed in Chapter 6).

The tightness of a binding is directly related to the amount of undyed fabric left after the fabric is dyed and the bindings are removed. Very tight binding produces areas of cloth that are dye-free. Looser binding allows small amounts of dye to penetrate the fabric. The combination of complete and incomplete penetration produces the gorgeous textures associated with this approach.

Only imagination limits the number of manipulations at your fingertips. Some lend themselves to smaller pieces of cloth, rather than to lengths of yardage. Others are versatile enough to be used on any expanse of fabric. Experiment with the suggested manipulations, and then explore ideas of your own. This is the first step in building a repertoire of patterns and textures that will be uniquely yours.

pleating, folding, scrunching, and making rings

These simple manipulations are quick and easy to do.

- ❖ **Pleat** the fabric. Experiment with the pleat widths. Roll the pleated fabric length jellyroll-style and secure it with a rubber band around the perimeter.

- ❖ **Fold** the fabric into a tight bundle. Larger lengths of fabric don't produce as much patterning as smaller pieces because the dye can't wick to the inside of the bundle.

- ❖ **Scrunch** the fabric by jamming it tightly into a length of old pantyhose. Don't tie a tight knot in the end. It can't escape! Untying wet pantyhose is a pain, so keep the knot loose.

- ❖ **Make rings** by pulling up points of fabric and wrap string or rubber bands around them. This is the classic tie-dye look from the 1960s. The end result is a series of spidery circles. It's especially gorgeous after one or more overdyes (see Chapter 2, Building Layers).

These basic manipulations generate a rich and varied set of background patterns. From the bottom right, they include (clockwise): flag fold between Plexiglas pieces, rubber-banded rings, pleated and rubber-banded cloth, cloth stuffed into a stocking, folded and rubber-banded cloth, cloth wrapped on a piece of PVC pipe.

flag fold

For this manipulation, you'll need a couple of small squares or rectangles of Plexiglas to hold the folded fabric.

❖ Begin by folding the fabric into four or more uniform pleats. The number of pleats will be determined by the size of the fabric and the width of the pleats you are folding.

❖ Iron the length of cloth to make the next set of folds easier to do.

❖ Fold one end of the fabric length on an angle, creating a triangle fold **(fig. 1)**.

❖ Fold the fabric again, at the diagonal created by the previous fold **(fig. 2)**. Whether you fold the triangle in toward the fold, or out away from it, you will get patterning, so don't worry about direction.

❖ Continue folding the fabric on the diagonal so that you make a series of triangles. The final bundle is a set of triangles "stacked" on top of each other **(fig. 3)**.

❖ Place Plexiglas pieces on the top and bottom of the triangular fold and secure them with rubber bands, prior to immersing the piece in a dyebath **(fig. 4)**.

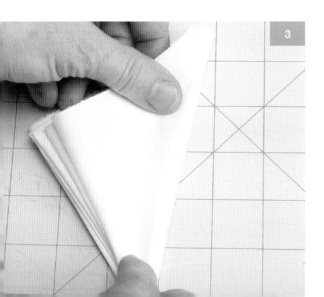

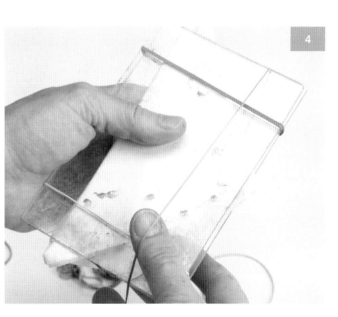

pole wrap

This manipulation is only suited to smaller pieces of cloth; see multiple pole wrapping, below, for a method suitable for larger pieces. Use a piece of PVC pipe from the home improvement store at least 4" (10 cm) in diameter. A 12" (30.5 cm) length is long enough for smaller pieces.

❖ Wrap the fabric around the pole, literally rolling it up on the pole. If the fabric is bigger than swatch size, fold it in half. Don't roll it too tight, or it will be difficult to scrunch down on the pole in the next step.

❖ After the fabric is rolled around the pipe, use a series of rubber bands stretched around the fabric on the pole to hold it in place. Do this by starting with a rubber band at the bottom, to keep the fabric from slipping off the pole. Add a new rubber band about an inch above the one at the end. As you add the second rubber band, slide the fabric toward the end of the pole, where the first rubber band is securing the cloth.

❖ Continue to add rubber bands about an inch apart; each time pushing the cloth toward the first rubber band at the end of the pole. When the last rubber band is secured, the entire piece of cloth should be scrunched to the end of the pole and secured by the series of rubber bands. The compacted fabric, paired with the tight resistance of the rubber bands, produces the patterning on the cloth.

❖ *Tip:* Put a thick rubber band on the pole near the end as a stopper. When the cloth is pushed down to the end of the pole, the rubber band will help keep it from popping off the pole.

Top: Pole wrap. Bottom: Using the multiple pole system creates even patterning across a longer fabric length.

multiple pole wrapping

This method, suitable for longer lengths of fabric, requires a sewing machine and a larger container for dyeing, as the multiple-pole bundle is significantly bigger than a single pole wrap or folded manipulation.

❖ Several pieces of PVC are needed for this technique. The poles should be the same length, preferably at least 18" (45.5 cm) long; different diameters are fine.

- Fold the yardage in half, with selvedges even. Slide a pole along the fold of the fabric. Determine how wide a channel to create to accommodate the pole. Allow an extra ½" (1.3 cm) ease. Mark the width of the channel on the fabric.

- Repeat this testing and measuring process until you have determined how many channels the cloth will accommodate, based on the width of the fabric and the size of the poles. Mark each channel **(fig. 1)**.

- Use a long machine basting stitch to form the channels, stitching from selvedge to selvedge **(fig. 2)**. Keep the lines of stitching straight and use the longest stitch possible so they'll be easy to remove later.

- Insert a pole into each channel you have sewn. Slide the fabric down the poles, easing it to make as compact a bundle as possible. The fabric stays in place due to a combination of the compacting and tightness of the channels **(fig. 3)**.

- Mix enough dye in a large container to accommodate the entire bundle of poles and fabric and dye according to instructions for immersion dyeing, page 46 **(fig. 4)**.

- When the dyebath is completed, remove poles and wash out fabric.

- Carefully remove the stitching after the cloth is dry.

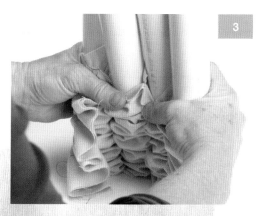

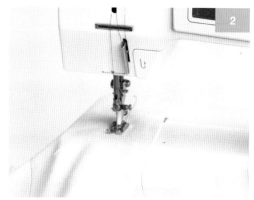

Printing on fabric with dye is compatible with a number of techniques, including, but not limited to, screenprinting, handpainting, stenciling, and stamping. All of these techniques fall into the general category of handprinted applications.

components for printing with dye

The non-negotiable chemicals are the same as for immersion dyeing; every handprinted application uses dye, water, and soda ash in the basic recipe. But some of the negotiable chemicals are different from those in an immersion dyebath. The following chemicals are used for handprinting applications.

Metaphos Metaphos (or Calgon) is optional, but it helps dye dissolve in hard water.

Soda ash While still a non-negotiable component, there are two ways to use soda ash as a fixer for printed applications. First, fabric can be soaked in soda ash solution prior to the application of dye. Second, soda ash can be added directly to the paste, activating the dye. Each has a benefit and a downside; see page 53.

Sodium alginate A seaweed based thickener, sodium alginate thickens the dye in the print paste, providing control over the application. There are two versions of sodium alginate sold by dye suppliers. One version is high viscosity (also known as SH alginate) meaning it has a thick consistency; the other is a low-viscosity sodium alginate product (F alginate), a thinner print consistency. Traditional dye printing practices recommend high-viscosity sodium alginate for cellulose fiber and the low-viscosity product for silk. Dye printing has changed, and *high-viscosity sodium alginate works for both protein and cellulose fibers*. It's the only product I ever buy and is worth the slightly higher price because less alginate is required to produce a perfect print mix.

Urea Urea is a humectant. It slows drying time and retains moisture so fabric and dye molecules have the maximum time to react. In damp climates, urea may be a negotiable component.

Print dye with stamps, stencils, or screens, or use a brush. Thickening the dye allows you to print clean, crisp design elements.

How to Use Soda Ash When Printing with Dye

Soda ash acts to fix the dye in both immersion dyeing and printing with dye. When printing with dye, soda ash can be used in two ways. First, fabric can be soaked in soda ash solution prior to the application of dye. Second, soda ash can be added directly to the paste, activating the dye.

Adding soda ash directly to the dye limits working time because the dye begins to exhaust as soon as the soda ash is added. Soaking cloth in soda ash prior to printing eliminates this issue. The dye doesn't exhaust, and working time is extended. Leftover dye without soda ash can keep for several days in the refrigerator.

The downside of a soda ash soak is that wet fabric must hang somewhere to dry. It can't be dried in the dryer; as the soda ash leaches into the machine, permeating clothing in the next dryer load, and it's itchy. **Note:** Iron soda ash-soaked fabric carefully. The soda ash scorches easily.

Adding soda ash to the dye/print mix limits working time, but it's my preferred method. I also use a special soda ash/baking soda blend, made from equal parts of the two chemicals. Baking soda slows the soda ash reaction time somewhat. I mix a 50/50 blend in a lidded plastic container, so it's ready whenever I want to print. When I start printing, I mix just enough activated print paste for the current project, so there is little waste at the end of the session. Once the soda ash is added to the dye, working time is about six hours. Some color remains available in the dye paste as long as four days after the soda ash is added to the dye, but the color is not as permanent as dye used within the suggested time frame.

Space and weather can affect the choice of one method over another. A blustery spring day is the perfect time to dry yards of soda ash-soaked fabric outdoors, and the fabric can be saved for several months. But if the weather outside is frightful, and inside studio space is limited, adding soda to the dye/print mix makes sense.

MAKING DYE PRINT PASTE

- 1 gallon (3.8 liters) of hot water
- ¾ cup (177 ml) urea
- 4–6 tablespoons (59–89 ml) ProThick SH*
- Soda ash
- Baking soda
- Dye
- Blender dedicated to dye-related mixing
- 2 one-gallon (3.8 liter) containers
- Measuring cup
- Measuring spoons
- Synthrapol

* ProThick SH is sodium alginate thickener. Use an amount that gives you the desired thickness of print paste. If the paste is too thick after it sets up, it can be thinned with activated chemical water (see Step 4).

This recipe makes one gallon of print paste—the thickened printing medium without the dye and soda ash. Make it 24 hours in advance of the first printing session so the chemicals dissolve completely. Covered print paste keeps in the refrigerator for several months so I always make at least a gallon, even if I won't use it all right away.

making dye print paste

1 Fill the blender half full of hot water from the premeasured gallon (3.8 liters). Begin blending with the lid on tightly **(fig. 1)**. Add half of the urea to the water in the blender. Also add two tablespoons (30 ml) of ProThick SH while the water/urea is blending. When the chemicals are dissolved, pour the blend into the empty gallon container **(fig. 2)**.

2 Continue mixing small batches of the ingredients until all of the hot water, urea, and sodium alginate have been used.

3 The print mix must sit for 30 to 40 minutes to set up, allowing any lumps to dissolve into the mix.

4 To make *activated* chemical water: Combine the ¾ cup (177 ml) urea, ⅓ cup (79 ml) soda ash, and 1 gallon of hot water without the thickener. It can be used for handpainted washes and to thin thick print paste prior to adding the dye.

5 When you're ready to mix dye with the print paste, put on your mask and gloves to work with dye powder.

6 Pour about 1 cup (237 ml) of print mix into a yogurt or other small container **(fig. 3)**.

7 Add 1 teaspoon (5 ml) soda ash fixative (50/50 mixture of soda ash and baking soda) **(fig. 4)**.

8 Add 1 teaspoon (5 ml) dye powder total (if you are mixing your own color, don't use more than 1 teaspoon (5 ml) total of dye colors combined) **(fig. 5)**. Mix thoroughly **(fig. 6)**.

Dye print paste can be screenprinted onto fabric, as described in Chapter 7.

working with dye print paste

Print paste with dye can be applied using all kinds of tools. Stamp, stencil, or screenprint, using the methods described in later chapters of this book, or simply draw, squirt, or doodle with the paste. Thin the print paste with the chemical water recipe described above if it needs to be runny enough to squirt through a bottle tip or applied with a brush.

Rolling dye-printed fabric or covering it with plastic insures moisture retention during batching.

batching dye-printed fabric

Once dye print paste has been applied, the fabric must be batched. Printed dyes require at least 24 hours for full reaction time, especially for blue and green dye colors. Red and yellow dyes strike faster than blue and green. Don't shortchange the color palette by washing out early; the intensity of the cooler colors will be compromised.

There are three keys to successful batching:

❖ *Time.* Give the cloth at least 24 hours.

❖ *Temperature.* The fabric must stay warm or the dye molecules will slow down and won't react completely. Keep the fabric warm (above 70°F [21°C]) by rolling it up in an old sheet or light plastic tablecloth. Put it near a heater or dryer. Bring it into the house if printing was done outdoors or in a garage. In cold climates, cover the plastic roll with an electric blanket.

❖ *Moisture.* The fabric must stay damp for the dyes to react properly. Rolling fabric or covering it with plastic ensures enough moisture retention to complete the dye reaction.

washing out dye-printed fabric

Ice is the secret ingredient! Unattached dye molecules can migrate onto parts of the printed or unprinted cloth where they would be most unwelcome. Ice in the wash out water bath shocks the unattached molecules and keeps them in suspension in the rinse water, preventing accidental bonding to the fabric where they aren't wanted.

1 Turn on the washing machine before you begin the initial rinse. Set it for a cold cycle and only use as much water as needed for the amount of fabric being rinsed.

2 Fill a five-gallon (19 liter) bucket half-full with cold water. Add two or three cups (474–711 ml) of ice cubes. This water/ice combination may be more or less than you need, based on the amount of fabric you're rinsing, so adapt accordingly.

3 Add 1 teaspoon (5 ml) of Synthrapol.

4 Wear gloves (the water is cold!) and plunge the fabric into the ice water. Swish it around for two or three minutes. Pour off the ice water.

5 Put the fabric in the washing machine. Add 1 teaspoon (5 ml) of Synthrapol. Let the cycle complete.

6 If the washing machine is equipped to go to a hot cycle at the end, let it run through the entire cycle. If setting cycles manually, set the final cycle to the hot water setting, when the cold cycle has completed. Rinsed cloth can be dried in the dryer or on a line.

TROUBLESHOOTING PRINTING WITH DYE

Most of the time, problems are operator error, so stay focused on process and follow the directions exactly. If problems occur at the end of the printed dye process, check these common causes.

pale color

Was soda ash included in the equation?

Did the fabric stay warm the entire 24 hours?

Was the 24-hour batching time observed?

Was there an adequate amount of dye in the print paste?

Was the print paste/dye combination fresh?

bleeding

Was printing clean at the start? Did the tool shift or blur, for example?

Did the cloth go into ice water before washing?

Did the wash cycle begin with a cold cycle and end with a hot cycle?

Did you overdo it when you added dye to the print paste? Too much dye is hard to wash out and readily migrates.

Example of printed dye bleeding on fabric.

TEXTILE PAINTS

Textile paints add color to fabric and are underrated tools in the layering toolbox. Paints got a bad rap in the past because older formulas dramatically changed the hand or drape of the fabric. Colors tended to shift slightly as the paint dried, presenting a challenge for inexperienced surface designers. Fast-forward twenty years, and paints are sophisticated revamps of past formulas—lightweight and sheer on fabric and permanent when dry. Best of all, paints feature qualities dyes don't possess and expand the layering repertoire.

Art cloth by Karen Harrison.

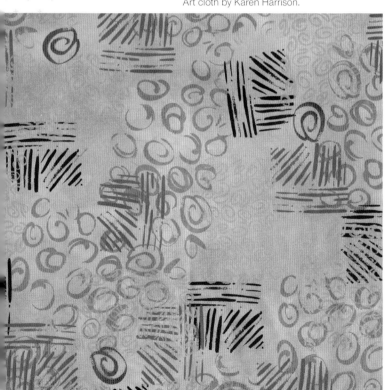

types of textile paints

Paints are not dyes. Textile paints are a mixture of pigment (color) and binder, the glue that holds the pigment to the surface. The binder is very similar to acrylic gel medium used by painters on stretched canvas. Binder may be thick or thin, translucent or opaque, but in every case it is essentially a plasticized coating that holds the pigment to the cloth permanently. Textile paint is related to other plastic/acrylic-based paints, including tube acrylic paints, craft and hobby acrylic paints, and even latex house paint, because the basic ingredients—pigment and binder—are essentially the same. It's the consistency of the paint and additional ingredients, such as softener, retarder (to slow drying time), and metallic components, that make textile paint unique.

Textile paint is formulated in four basic styles, and the style is directly related to the binder.

There is a wide range of paint types and styles available to textile artists and each paint has its own unique qualities.

translucent

Translucent textile paints produce a sheer layer of color on the cloth. The binder is opaque while wet, but upon drying becomes translucent, allowing background color, and anything printed under the paint, to be visible. Different brands of textile paint exhibit different levels of translucency. Some are a sheer glaze of color while others are slightly more opaque. Paints are translucent unless the label (or catalog) says *opaque*. Test paints before incorporating them into a layering project, because translucent paint reveals underlying colors and images as it dries. Testing eliminates the dismay and disappointment of recognizing too late that a poor choice was made, with no hope of removing paint and starting again.

opaque

Opaque textile paints don't turn translucent as the paint dries. A chalk-like ingredient in the formula ensures that the paint retains its opacity. Opaque paints cover completely, so they're a good choice for dark backgrounds. The color also stays true after drying, although a test is still in order, as sometimes the color lightens slightly during the drying phase. Opaque paints change the hand of the fabric more than other fabric paints because the ingredients that make them opaque are heavier than those in translucent paints, thus adding some stiffness.

metallic

Metallic textile paints include ingredients such as mica to give the paint a shiny, metallic finish. The binder is translucent. Available in a wide array of colors, metallic paints are intermixable with translucent or opaque paints. Paints stay visible on dark fabrics because the metallic components are finely ground, but not so finely ground as to sink into the surface and disappear.

These green paints vary widely in color, coverage, and consistency. *Top row, left to right:* Setacolor Transparent Textile Paint #27 Light Green; Setacolor Transparent Textile Paint #15 Emerald Green; Setacolor Opaque Textile Paint #27 Light Green. *Middle row, left to right:* Versatex Textile Paint #316 Green; Neopaque Textile Paint #587 Green; PROChem PROFab Opaque Textile Paint #70 Kelly Green. *Third Row:* PROChem PROFab Textile Paint #70 Kelly Green; PROChem PROFab Textile Paint #72 Emerald; Jacquard Textile Color #117 Emerald Green. *Bottom Row:* Jacquard Textile Color #116 Apple Green.

watercolor-weight

Watercolor-weight textile paints are designed to mimic dye. The acrylic binder is as thin as water, limiting the paints to specific applications. Watercolor paints can't be stenciled or screen-printed because they bleed and won't hold a clean edge, but they are great for stamping, spraying with a misting bottle, or using as dye on folded and manipulated applications. Apply paint to the fabric with a brush, rather than immersing the fabric in a container of paint. No batching time is required as no chemical reaction occurs.

working with
textile paint extender

To alter the characteristics of a paint, it may seem like a good idea to water down thicker paint, rather than investing in another product, but it's a false economy. Watercolor-weight paints are designed to stay in suspension, which means the pigment won't separate from the liquid binder and sink to the bottom of the container. Watering down thick paint leads to separation of pigment and binder resulting from the added water. It's a fast way to clog a spray bottle and also problematic during printing, when the added water has a tendency to leech away from the printed pigment and halo around it.

Textile paint extender is a product that can be used to make transparent color more sheer, or opaque paint lighter in color. Extender consists of paint base or binder, minus the pigment. There are several varieties of extender, and each is related to a particular paint type.

- Translucent extender dries clear and matte on the surface of the cloth.
- Opaque extender dries opaque white.
- Metallic extender is a translucent binder with metallic components but no pigment.

Extender is useful because it can be mixed into any pigmented paint. Adding binder without pigment stretches the amount of pigment over more volume and makes color sheerer (in the case of translucent paint) without actually thinning the paint. If the goal is a sheer glaze of color, extender is a better choice than adding water and running the risk of separation or haloing.

Adding extender to opaque paint makes the color lighter rather than sheerer. Adding metallic extender maintains the metallic quality of the surface while lightening the overall color of the original paint. Since extenders are all related, they can be intermixed with each other and with all of the other paints. For example, if the opaque paint on my shelf is too thick for the fabric I intend to print, I can add translucent extender to it. The paint will still be a great consistency for printing, but it won't be quite as opaque and heavy as it was originally.

Manufacturers specializing in paints other than textile paints sell a "textile medium" and promote adding it to acrylic paint to make the paint suitable for fabric. In general, this is not a good idea. It might be fine for T-shirt printing, but if your interests run to refined printed imagery on high-end fabrics, the effect will be inferior. Choose the best textile paint and paint extenders that you can afford. It does make a difference!

recommended paint brands
from my toolbox

You will develop your own paint preferences, but here are a few of my favorites at the time of this book's publication. See Resources, page 173, for suppliers.

Watercolor Paint Brands I like Dye-Na-Flow by Jacquard. These paints are loaded with pigment and mimic dye beautifully. They are the consistency of thin milk, but even with additional water the colors are vivid and true. Pebeo's SetaSilk is a close second but slightly more expensive. Sometimes color choice guides a purchase; both companies make sophisticated colors, and remember, the paints can be intermixed.

Transparent or Translucent Paint Brands PRO-fab by PRO Chemical & Dye is one of the best values around; they're highly pigmented and offer an extensive collection of colors. This brand stocks my toolbox because the colors are vivid, reliable, and cost-effective. Setacolor is also a reliable choice for this particular style of paint. The colors are saturated, but the price point is slightly higher than the PROfab line.

A selection of textile paints.

Opaque Paint Brands PROfab is again a favorite, but sometimes this brand is heavy on the hand of the fabric. Setacolor Opaque paints are softer and not as dense. In my opinion, this is the category of paint that needs improvement. No brand is completely opaque on black, and all affect the hand of the fabric. But this is an area where innovations occur all the time, so keep trying out new paints.

Metallic Paint Brands For me, Setacolor wins hands down when it comes to metallic pigment load. The paints are creamy, highly metallic, and soft to the touch.

Try various brands of textile paints.

COLOR AND TEXTILE PAINTS

Acquiring and studying paints is a long-term project all by itself. Buy basic color wheel matches based on my advice and then acquire other colors that appeal to your own sensibility. Expect to explore this topic again and again in a quest for understanding that will eventually make paint selection a breeze.

Colored pigments are imperfect. Few pigments are an exact match to the basic primary, secondary, and tertiary colors on the color wheel, because most pigments have an overtone, a secondary cast of color that affects our perception of a color as either *warm* or *cool*. Every color except the basic twelve on a simple color wheel leans toward either the warm end of the spectrum (yellow, orange, red) or the cool end of the spectrum (blue, green, purple). Sometimes you can't tell which way a color leans unless you compare it to another version of the same color, so it's important to recognize how relative colors are to each other.

The potential for an overtone of color to be hidden in a paint formula can make paint mixing complicated. The label may say *blue*, but how do you know the blue you are planning to mix with red doesn't have a green overtone? If it does, you will never be able to mix that gorgeous purple you have in mind.

To discover whether paint color has a hidden overtone, mix it with white textile paint. Most of the time, the overtones assert themselves when the white paint is added. Then the color can be adjusted by adding small amounts of another color, to compensate for the overtone.

The terms *jewel tone* and *earth tone* are terms sometimes used to refer to both dye colors and paint colors. Jewel-tone colors are comparable to the colors used to print paper. They are clear and bright and mix to create clear, bright secondary colors. Earth tone colors are earthier, with rich, subtle overtones.

Mixed earth-tone colors generate great secondary colors, but the colors are not as pure and bright as those achieved by mixing the jewel-tone set. To effectively mix the widest range of paint colors (which also allows matching almost any color fabric from a dyebath), it's worth owning both an earth-tone primary set and a jewel-tone primary set of paints.

It may also be a good idea to own sets of primaries in both translucent and opaque versions. Better make some shelf space and get out the credit card! Yes, it could be a challenge to assemble, store, and pay for all of these paints, but it's the only way to make truly accurate color matching possible.

Most catalogs indicate which paint the company considers the jewel- or earth-tone colors. If in doubt, contact the company and ask them. Most suppliers are happy to help. And don't forget to order white, black, and a few metallic colors, too.

The colors on the right—sun yellow, turquoise, and fuchsia or magenta—are jewel-tone colors. They are warm primaries and mix to create bright, clear colors. The colors on the left—golden yellow, blue, and red—are earth-tone primaries. They combine to produce secondary colors that are deep and saturated.

Several beautiful versions of green can be mixed by combining different amounts of sun yellow, turquoise, golden yellow, and blue. *Top row, left to right:* sun yellow + blue; golden yellow + blue. *Bottom row, left to right:* sun yellow + turquoise; golden yellow + turquoise.

These examples of mixed orange illustrate the wide range of color possible by mixing two primary sets of red and yellow. *Top row, left to right:* golden yellow + magenta; golden yellow + red. *Bottom row, left to right:* sun yellow + magenta; sun yellow + red.

WORKING WITH TEXTILE PAINTS

Textile paints are suitable for stamping, stenciling, screenprinting, Thermofax printing, and handpainting. Success depends on printing technique as much as paint products. Consult the individual chapters that follow for advice about using these techniques. The following is a general overview of paint use.

✦ Keep your paints tightly capped and stored away from extremes of heat or cold.

✦ You can mix paints with varying weights, styles, and opacities, based on what the painting or printing project requires. Store leftover paint in tightly capped containers to prevent it from drying out.

✦ Since paint is permanent when dry, be sure to wash your tools as soon as the printing session ends. Follow the manufacturer's instructions for cleaning.

✦ If a print is unsatisfactory, you might be able to wash it out quickly, depending on the paint. A ghost image may remain, so then there will be a new design element to consider!

✦ Never iron paint to dry it out. The composition is affected by heat, and the paint gets rubbery.

✦ Paints air-cure in about two weeks if the fabric isn't washed in the interim. If you need to wash the fabric sooner, the paint must be heat-set by ironing the dry paint with an iron set on the high/linen/cotton setting, if the fabric will tolerate it. If necessary, use a press cloth to protect the fabric from heat damage.

✦ Iron each paint layer after it dries, following the manufacturer's instructions. Paint adheres better to new paint if the layers are heat-set by ironing as the project evolves. At the finish, minimal ironing will be required. As a rule of thumb, the fabric should be very hot to the touch. Continue across the cloth until the entire surface is heated.

✦ Tumbling fabric in a hot dryer contributes to the heat-setting process, but in my experience it isn't a substitute for ironing. Heating fabric in a microwave or oven is risky. Heat won't penetrate the fabric evenly, and there's some possibility of starting a fire. Either heat-set the paint by ironing or observe the two-week waiting period, during which time the paint air-cures.

Art cloth by Maggie Weiss.

TROUBLESHOOTING TEXTILE PAINT PROBLEMS

Sometimes things don't always go as planned when painting. Here are some common occurrences and typical causes.

paint bleeds or runs

❖ Was too much paint applied to the fabric?

❖ Was water added to the paint that wicked away from the design while it was drying?

paint washes out in the washing machine

❖ Was the paint heat-set or air-cured properly?

Left to right: Paint bled because water was added to it; paint washed off because it wasn't properly heat-set; paint was applied too thickly, stiffening the feel of the fabric.

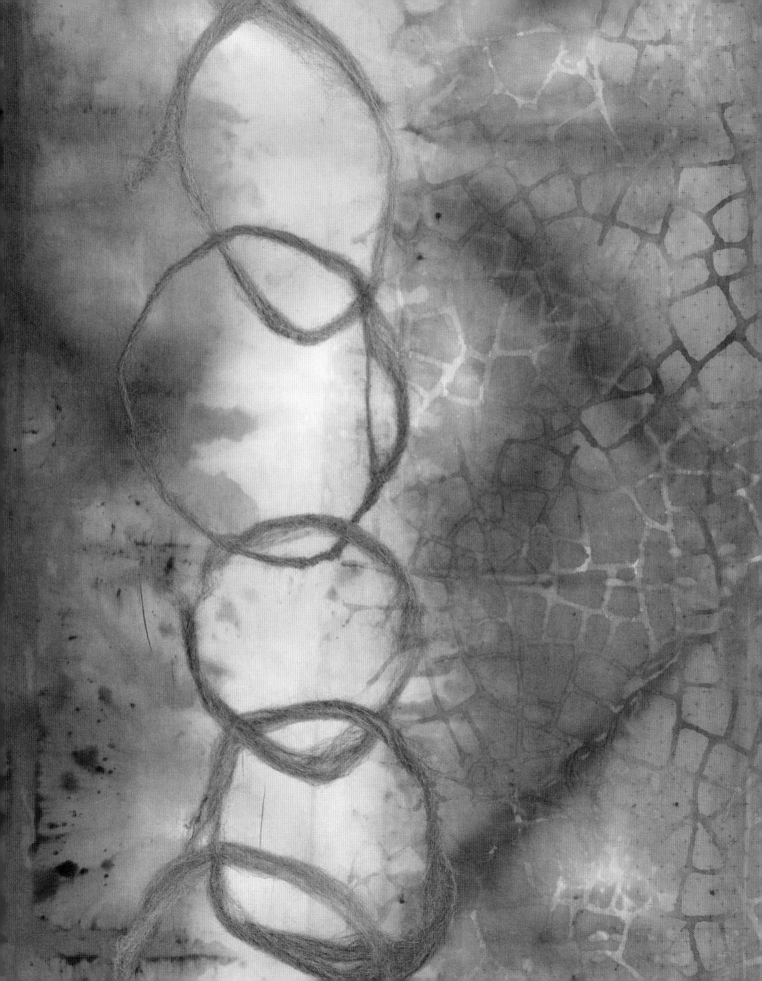

removing color:
discharge methods

Discharging is the removal of color through a chemical reaction, orchestrated by applying substances to dyed fabric to strip color, either completely or partially. When it's carefully controlled, discharging generates effective contrast and shading as a component of the layering process. In this chapter, we'll see how discharging is a ready companion to both resists and textile paints, and has the added bonus of maintaining the original hand of the fabric.

Understanding the Discharge Process :: Discharge Agent :: Chlorine Bleach :: Jacquard Discharge Paste
Rit Color Remover :: Thiourea Dioxide :: Adding Discharge Samples :: Troubleshooting

Detail, Chain Reaction, Jane Dunnewold, 2008.
Cotton, manipulated, dyed, overdyed, discharged,
screenprinted, with needlefelting.

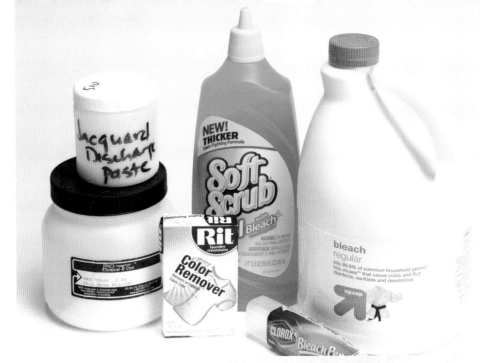

Always use care with discharge products.

CAUTION:
Safety First

Discharge agents are among the most hazardous chemicals that fiber artists encounter. Each of us must decide what level of risk to accept when choosing to discharge or not and which chemicals to utilize. I cannot emphasize enough the importance of responsible use of these products. Not every discharge agent is described as hazardous, but human beings have individual sensitivities to chemicals. A process or product that doesn't have an impact on me could affect you.

▲ Monitor your body and your reaction to chemicals while working and recognize your responsibility to those around you, whether classmates, children, or family pets.

▲ Don't discharge in a studio with a ventilation system that circulates fumes throughout the building.

▲ Plan studio time and space carefully.

▲ Wear a respirator and gloves.

▲ Use a box fan to force fumes out of the immediate environment—preferably out the window—or work outdoors when weather permits.

▲ Dispose of the chemicals by diluting with water and pour the mix down the drain at the end of the work session (discharge chemicals don't damage septic systems or plumbing).

There are two types of discharging agents. The first, which includes all chlorine bleach products, works through oxidation, a chemical reaction in which electrons are removed from atoms in a molecule. The second type, which includes thiourea dioxide (thiox), Jacquard Discharge Paste, Formusol, and Rit Color Remover, works by reduction, a chemical reaction in which electrons are added.

All reductive discharge agents contain sulfur dioxide, the chemical responsible for the color changes during the discharging process. Reductive discharge chemicals require heat to activate the reaction that breaks the double bonds in the dye chemicals. Some recipes call for hot water in the washing machine; most call for the higher temperatures of a discharge bath heated in a cooking pot, or heated with a steamer or steam iron.

factors affecting successful discharging

Only dyed fabrics can be discharged. Discharge chemicals don't affect textile paints because paint is stable pigment suspended in a plastic binder. No chemical reaction occurs when paint is subjected to a discharge agent. Color stripping of dyed fabric is directly related to three factors:

❖ **Temperature.** Applying heat, as described above, is required for reductive agents only. *Never apply heat to a chlorine discharge.*

❖ **Time.** Changes in color are directly related to the length of time that the fabric is exposed to the discharge agent. Whether you are ironing a printed discharge agent, immersing the fabric in a discharge bath, or subjecting it to a chlorine solution through printing or immersion, time is a factor.

❖ **Dyestuff.** Even within a single category of dyes, such as MX fiber-reactive dyes, some colors discharge more effectively than others. Certain dye colors won't discharge at all because of chemical composition. Test the discharging agent against the intended dye color. Testing determines not only dischargeability, but also the color that will result from the discharging application. Knowing what result a discharge process will produce is critical to planning color-layering sequences.

stabilizing the fabric after discharging

Stabilizing fabric after applying discharge agents means *removing chemical residue from the fabric completely.* This is important for three reasons:

❖ If left in the cloth, the discharging agent will cause damage over time.

❖ The discharging agent may react to chemicals you introduce during the next step of coloring or patterning the cloth. This further chemical reaction can damage the fabric, but more important, it can be hazardous to humans. Adding one process to another without first stabilizing the fabric is potentially dangerous.

❖ Discharge agents are smelly, and ironed applications can make the fabric stiff. Washing eliminates odors and returns the cloth to its original hand.

CHOOSING AND USING DISCHARGE AGENTS

Your choice of discharge agent will be influenced by the style and type of your fabric and by whether your intention is printed imagery, selective stripping of color, or total stripping of color.

⋄ Chlorine bleach can only be used on fabric made from cellulose plant fibers (cotton, linen, hemp, rayon). Protein fibers, including silk and wool, are not candidates for bleach.

⋄ Reductive discharge agents are more versatile, lending themselves to applications on both cellulose and protein fibers. If your layering strategy dictates discharging a fabric more than once, always stabilize the cloth between applications.

⋄ Prewash all fabric in hot water with a perfume-free, additive-free laundry detergent before discharging.

⋄ Always apply the discharging agent according to directions specific to the chemical. Read the manufacturer's instructions. Neutralize as required by the individual agent. Wash the fabric in warm water and a mild detergent prior to continued color application or completion of the cloth.

Discussion of individual discharge agents follows.

Samples of discharged fabric show variations in color changes.

About Antichlor

Antichlor, a chemical specifically designed to neutralize chlorine bleach, is available from dye supply companies. Antichlor effectively counteracts chlorine but has its own hazards. For those who prefer not to use antichlor, I suggest the shoebox test. Fold up dried fabric after washing and stabilizing. Put it in a shoebox overnight. If you can smell bleach later, when the lid is removed, the fabric needs another wash and rinse in cold water and detergent. Simple, but effective!

If you choose to use antichlor, follow these guidelines:

❖ Antichlor is an irritant. Those with asthma should avoid it.

❖ Wear a mask when mixing antichlor with water.

❖ Always add antichlor to cold water, never warm or hot water.

❖ Always rinse fabric discharged with bleach before putting it into an antichlor bath.

❖ Change the antichlor water after using it to neutralize several lengths of fabric.

❖ Dispose of solution at the end of the discharging session. Don't save it.

Always rinse excess bleach out of the fabric before immersing the cloth in an antichlor bath.

instructions for neutralizing with antichlor

1 Rinse discharged fabric in cool running water and wring it out.

2 Soak fabric for 10 minutes in a solution of 1 teaspoon (5 ml) of antichlor mixed into 1 gallon (3.8 liters) of cold water.

3 Wash the fabric in the cool cycle in the washing machine. No additional soap is required for the final wash and rinse.

4 Dispose of the antichlor solution after use.

CHLORINE BLEACH (sodium hypochlorite)

Contrary to popular opinion, chlorine bleach is *not* safer than other discharging chemicals. In part because we assume that household products are safe, chlorine bleach probably has the potential to be more harmful than other discharge agents. It's essential to work carefully and follow all safety precautions.

❖ Always work in an area with good ventilation.

❖ Never spray a chlorine product inside the studio.

❖ Use chlorine bleach on cellulose fibers only (cotton, linen, rayon, hemp, and blends of those fibers). Bleach won't discharge synthetic fabrics, so experimenting with them is simply wasted time and effort.

❖ Prewash commercial fabric intended for bleaching. The sizing applied to fabric to make it look smooth and neat on the bolt has the potential to interact with chlorine, and the resulting fumes can make you sick.

❖ Establish the good habit of testing prior to purchase. Cellulose fabric dyed with fiber reactive MX dye usually discharges easily, but a few colors are resistant. Test to determine the suitability of bleaching, the resulting color, and the speed of the lightening process.

❖ Sometimes a cotton fabric won't discharge, perhaps because the fabric was treated with a chemical to eliminate the risk of fading over time. Some commercially applied dyes resist discharging.

❖ Choosing a thickened product offers greater control of printed applications and slows reaction time, which translates into more working time for you. Products such as Soft Scrub, Clorox Gel bleach, and Sunlight dishwasher gel are examples of thickened household cleaners that contain bleach.

❖ If you select liquid bleach, you can thin it with water in a 50/50 ratio. Don't add water to thickened chlorine products, as the thickness is the reason to choose them over straight chlorine. Always test first to avoid disaster and disappointment.

❖ Watch the bleaching action closely as you work. Thickened products discharge more slowly than straight bleach applications.

Whether applying bleach directly or printing with a thickened product, wash out the fabric in cool running water when the desired lightness is achieved. Pay attention to printed areas and try not to let them touch, or migration of the bleaching agent can occur.

Dyed fabrics are pleated, bound, and ready for discharging.

PROCESS:
DISCHARGING BOUND-RESIST FABRICS WITH CHLORINE BLEACH

Chlorine bleach is available in the concentrated laundry version and also as a pre-thickened cleaner. Both products have versatile applications.

discharging bound-resist fabrics with chlorine bleach

1 Fold, wrap, or otherwise manipulate the fabric, using the bound-resist methods described on page 48.

2 Apply bleach. This is best done with a foam brush rather than by immersing the fabric **(fig. 1 and fig. 2)**. Work quickly and never step away from the discharged cloth.

3 Remove bindings and wash in cool water immediately **(fig. 3)**.

4 If desired, neutralize the cloth in a bath of 1 teaspoon (5 ml) of antichlor mixed into 1 gallon (3.8 liters) of cold water (see sidebar, page 71).

5 Wash in cool water in the washing machine.

- Cellulose fabric (cotton, linen, ramie, or rayon)
- T-pins
- Padded printing surface
- Thickened bleach product
- *Tools:* Foam brushes, stencils, stamps, Thermofax screens, silkscreens other than photo-emulsion screens
- Water

Optional: antichlor

It is possible to make your own thickened chlorine bleach product with Monagum powder thickener, available from dye suppliers. However, Monagum is not as effective as commercially thickened household bleach products, such as Soft Scrub, Clorox Gel, and Sunlight dishwasher gel. Choose these household products for reliable consistency and longer working time. Be sure to check the expiration date prior to purchase.

printing with chlorine discharge agents

1 Pin dry fabric to the printing surface with T-pins.

2 Apply a thickened bleach product with stamps, stencils, Thermofax screens, silkscreens, or by handpainting with a foam brush. Work quickly and never step away from the discharged cloth.

3 When color change is satisfactory, rinse the fabric in cool water.

4 If desired, neutralize the cloth in a bath of 1 teaspoon (5 ml) of antichlor mixed into 1 gallon (3.8 liters) of cold water (see sidebar, page 71).

5 Wash in cool water in the washing machine.

Left to right: Brush bleach onto a stamp; stamp repeatedly to discharge an overall pattern; print a thickened bleach product through a Thermofax or other silkscreen.

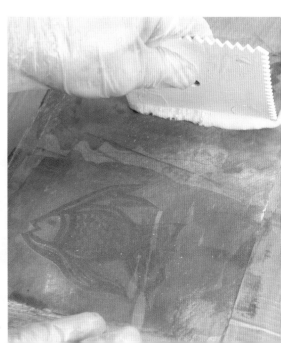

JACQUARD DISCHARGE PASTE

Art cloth by Kathleen McTee shows the depth made possible with Jacquard Discharge Paste on silk.

The active ingredient in Jacquard Discharge Paste, manufactured by the Jacquard Company, is Rongalite. This effective discharging agent is used as an industrial bleaching agent and compound for commercial dyeing. Similar products are sold as Rongalite, formusol, sodium hydroxymethane sulfinate, sodium formaldehye sulfoxylate, and several other names. Guidelines for use:

❖ Jacquard Discharge Paste is designed for natural fibers.

❖ Always wear a respirator and gloves when applying Jacquard Discharge Paste. A cavalier attitude toward safety with this product can lead to health issues, which are easily avoided if proper safety measures are observed.

❖ Jacquard Discharge Paste is premixed and relatively stable, although prolonged exposure to heat causes the paste to break down. Thin paste should be discarded. Once the consistency is compromised, it won't hold a clean edge during printing.

❖ Reserve Jacquard Discharge Paste for printed applications.

❖ Always test in advance. Occasionally a fabric looks as though it discharged but after washing, the color returns to the original state. In such a case, the paste changes color, giving the illusion that the original dye color changed. In fact, the paste didn't effectively strip color from the cloth to which it was applied. This phenomenon is related to the manufacturer's dye, as some dye categories are not amenable to discharging by Rongalite.

❖ Don't apply discharge paste to any fabric that can't be washed out (stabilized) later. The product is smelly and stiffens fabric. However, both qualities disappear when the cloth is washed.

❖ Never thin Jacquard Discharge Paste with water. Thinning reduces the ability of the product to discharge the cloth.

❖ Discharge paste is most effective when applied to dry cloth and then heated while it is still damp. Don't wait for the paste to dry. On smooth, lightweight fabrics, such as silk habotai, the printed edges will blur if the product dries prior to steaming. The ability of the agent to lighten also diminishes.

❖ Some artists have found that exposure to sunlight enhances the ability of discharge paste to remove color, reducing ironing or steaming time.

PRINTING WITH JACQUARD DISCHARGE PASTE

- Dyed fabric made of natural fibers, either cellulose (cotton, linen, rayon) or protein (silk)
- Jacquard Discharge Paste
- Respirator
- *Tools:* Stamps, stencils, Thermofax screens, silkscreens, brushes
- Steam iron
- Damp towel
- Padded surface
- Water
- Fan

This approach to printing allows you to print an image and heat an image, print an image and heat an image. The wet paste can be activated and dried one element at a time, so it doesn't smear when a new image is layered over a previous one. The artist controls whether a printed image is lightened as much as possible, or stopped while some color remains—a useful aspect of building layers and the illusion of depth.

If possible, reserve an iron specifically for discharging. I ruined one of my mother's blouses by offering her an iron I'd just that afternoon used for discharging. Yikes! Not a pretty picture.

printing with jacquard discharge paste

1 Wearing a respirator, and using a fan to pull chemical fumes away from you, apply Jacquard Discharge Paste to dry stable fabric that you've tested for discharge-ability with this product, using the tools of your choice (fig. 1).

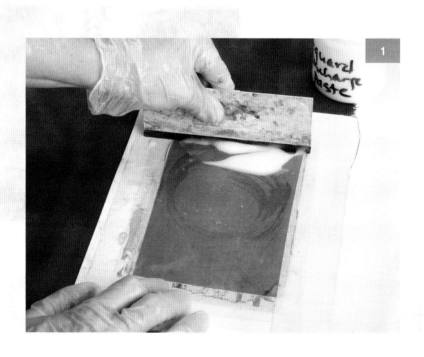

2 Wearing a respirator, heat the damp discharge paste with a steam iron set on high. Use plenty of steam. Pounce the iron up and down over the damp paste, drying it out slightly before setting the iron down on the cloth surface. Positioning the iron over damp paste without moving it up and down results in marks from the vent holes, which aren't easily disguised **(fig. 2)**.

3 To protect your discharging iron, dampen an old towel and fold it in half. Put it next to the iron on the ironing board or worktable. Use it to wipe off the bottom of the iron as you work. The damp terry cloth "scrubs" the iron after each image is heated and keeps the discharge paste from sticking and burning on the bottom of the iron **(fig. 3)**.

4 Once the initial drying occurs, it's acceptable to put the iron on the fabric and steam it vigorously. The additional shots of steam continue to remove color.

5 When the entire fabric is discharged, stabilize it by washing it in cool water with mild soap, to remove odor and chemical residue. Discharged cloth can be kept unwashed for some time; it will still smell, but there isn't any hazard to the fabric by waiting to wash it out.

6 Dye or overdye fabric immediately after stabilizing or discharge additional images using the paste or another agent. Never apply a second discharging agent to fabric that hasn't been stabilized. To do so may result in a hazardous chemical reaction.

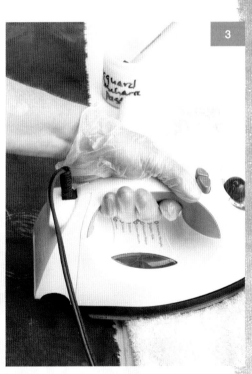

RIT COLOR REMOVER

Available in grocery and drugstores, Rit Color Remover (a brand equivalent of sodium hydrosulfite, sodium dithionite, and sodium sulfoxylate) is easy to use in the washing machine or in a stovetop enamel pot. The discharged color that Rit produces is different from that generated by other discharge agents, adding to its appeal for makers of art cloth. Follow these guidelines:

❖ While Rit Color Remover is easy to use, it is absolutely necessary to wear a respirator and gloves and to have good ventilation in the work space.

❖ Rit Color Remover is designed primarily for immersion applications and is not suitable for printing.

❖ Package directions suggest adding Rit Color Remover to hot water in the washing machine, but you'll achieve a more dramatic color change by heating the solution in an enamel pan on a hot plate and immersing the fabric briefly.

❖ Mix about as much solution as is needed to saturate the fabric(s), since extra solution must be discarded at the end of the work session. Preparing a Rit Color Remover bath is not related to the weight of fabric.

❖ Be aware of these disadvantages to Rit Color Remover and other sodium hydrosulfite products:

- **Limited color capability.** With this product, many fiber-reactive MX dye colors discharge to versions of yellow, yellow-green, and orange, regardless of original color. Test, test, test.

- **Limited overdyeing ability.** A number of fiber-reactive MX dye colors resist overdyeing with another MX color after being discharged with Rit Color Remover, due to chemical changes in the fabric.

- **No neutralizing agent.** There is no available neutralizing agent to aid subsequent overdyeing of the discharged cloth.

- **Short working time.** The discharge bath begins to exhaust as soon as it is heated and exposed to air.

Fabric dyed, discharged, and finished with foil.

PROCESS:
DISCHARGING BOUND-RESIST FABRICS WITH RIT COLOR REMOVER

SUPPLIES

- Respirator
- Heavy rubber gloves
- Fan
- Dyed fabric
- Rubber bands, string, Plexiglas
- Rit Color Remover
- Large enamel or stainless steel pot (dedicated to discharging)
- Wooden spoon (dedicated to discharging)
- Wooden tongs (dedicated to discharging)
- Stove or hot plate
- Cold water

Incorporating Rit Color Remover into a layered printing plan for art cloth is not what the manufacturers envisioned, so adopt an experimental approach to the use of this product and keep notes to help you reproduce results.

discharging bound-resist fabrics with rit color remover

1 Prepare fabric for immersion by binding, folding, pleating, etc., using the guidelines on page 48. Use rubber bands or string to secure the manipulations **(fig. 1)**.

2 Add one package of Rit Color Remover to one gallon of cold water in a stainless steel or enamel pot dedicated to this use. No equipment used in the kitchen should ever be used for dyeing or discharging processes. Do not add the Rit Color Remover powder to hot water. Stir it into cold water until the powder dissolves and wear a respirator while mixing.

3 Heat the discharge solution on a hot plate, preferably outdoors or near an open window with a fan blowing fumes away from the room and out the open window. Working in the garage is another alternative. Wear a respirator during the heating and immersing process. A dust mask is not adequate protection from the sulfur dioxide fumes! Bring the discharge bath just barely to simmer. It should not actively boil, as boiling reduces the amount of liquid quickly and limits working time. If the water is steaming, it's hot enough.

4 Wear heavy rubber gloves or use wooden tongs to dip the manipulated fabric bundle into the hot discharge solution **(fig. 2)**. Heavy gloves provide more control over the process.

5 Dip the fabric quickly and watch for color change, which is usually fast. Err on the side of too little time in the bath, as fabric can be immersed again to remove more color, but color can't be easily added back **(fig. 3)**.

6 Move immediately to the sink. Rinse the fabric in cold water while removing bindings. Unfold or pull apart the fabric so cold water soaks the entire piece of cloth **(fig. 4)**. Rinse fabric thoroughly.

7 Finish in the washing machine with a single rinse and spin cycle. No additional soap is required for stabilization.

8 Dry the fabric in the dryer. The final color of the discharged cloth isn't stable until the fabric is dry. Keep records to limit variables and increase predictability.

9 If the discharging action slows after repeated use, pour out the remaining chemical solution and mix a new bath. At the end of your discharging session, pour out and dispose of unused solution, as it cannot be used again.

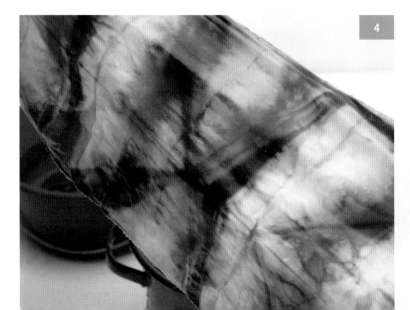

THIOUREA DIOXIDE
(thiox)

Thiourea dioxide is a popular discharging agent manufactured in China, where it is sold primarily to whiten and brighten paper pulp for recycling and re-use; it's often abbreviated as thiox and is also sold under the name Spectralite. Thiourea dioxide is a powdered stable compound that dissolves in water and decomposes gradually, during which time the discharging action occurs. Guidelines for use:

* Not without its hazards, thiox should be used in a protected environment. It is absolutely necessary to use a respirator, rubber gloves, and adequate ventilation.

* Thiox applications will successfully discharge both cellulose (cotton, linen, hemp, rayon) and protein (silk, wool) fibers.

* Prepare thiox as an immersion bath or as a printed means of color removal/alteration.

* The chemical reaction is promoted by the application of heat.

* Reaction time with thiox is slower than with Rit Color Remover and is particularly affected by a weakly alkaline climate; this is why soda ash is included in the recipe suggested for discharging cloth.

Discharged elements can be subtle or dramatic.

PROCESS:
DISCHARGING
CELLULOSE-FIBER CLOTH WITH
THIOX IMMERSION

SUPPLIES

- Respirator
- Heavy gloves, such as the upper-arm-length gloves from PRO Chemical & Dye
- Fan
- Fabric made from cellulose fiber (cotton, linen, hemp, rayon)
- Thiourea dioxide powder
- Soda ash
- Measuring spoons
- Measuring cup
- Bucket
- Large enamel or stainless steel pot (dedicated to discharging)
- Wooden spoon or tongs (dedicated to discharging)
- Stove or hot plate
- Rubber bands or string for making bound resists

Remember to sample discharge results to determine the final color in advance of discharging a length of cloth. It's useful to be able to predict color changes early in the design and coloration process.

discharging cellulose-fiber cloth with thiox immersion

1 Manipulate fabric by folding, pleating, or using other methods of bound resist (see page 48).

2 On the stove or hot plate, heat two gallons of water in an enamel or stainless steel pot, to just under a simmer, about 180°F (82°C).

3 Wearing a respirator and gloves, and with a fan to pull chemical fumes away from you, add 3 teaspoons (15 ml) of thiox and 2 tablespoons (30 ml) of soda ash.

4 Immediately add the bound fabric. The length of time the fabric is in the bath is variable and is based on the fabric content, the original fabric dye, and the desired amount of color removal. Don't walk away from the bath when the fabric is immersed. Dip the manipulated fabric into the bath using a gloved hand. If selectively removing color, dip the cloth into the bath and then lift it to check the color change. To remove all color, leave the fabric in the thiox bath longer.

5 Lift out the cloth and check for color change (fig. 1). Dip again as needed.

6 To stabilize thiox-immersed fabric, rinse fabric in cool water. If not enough color is removed, rinse and dry the cloth and treat it again.

7 You can overdye cellulose fibers without any further neutralization treatment.

8 The thiox is replete if you can smell ammonia. The immersion bath can be reactivated once or twice by adding 3 teaspoons [15 ml] additional thiox. Do not add more soda ash.

1

PROCESS:
DISCHARGING
PROTEIN-FIBER CLOTH WITH
THIOX IMMERSION

The process for discharging wool, silk, or other protein-based fiber in a thiox immersion bath is the same as for cellulose fibers. However, the stabilization process includes the addition of white vinegar.

discharging protein-fiber cloth with thiox immersion

1 Manipulate fabric by folding, pleating, or using other methods of bound resist (see page 48).

2 On the stove or hot plate, heat two gallons of water in an enamel or stainless steel pot, to just under a simmer, about 180°F (82°C).

3 Wearing a respirator and gloves and with a fan to pull chemical fumes away from you, add 3 teaspoons (15 ml) of thiox and 2 tablespoons (30 ml) of soda ash.

4 Immediately add the bound fabric. The length of time the fabric is in the bath is variable and is based on the fabric content, the original fabric dye, and the desired amount of color removal. Don't walk away from the bath when the fabric is immersed. Dip the manipulated fabric into the bath using a gloved hand. If selectively removing color, dip the cloth into the bath and then lift it to check the color change. To remove all color, leave the fabric in the thiox bath longer.

5 Lift out the cloth and check for color change (fig. 1). Dip again as needed.

6 To stabilize the fabric, rinse it in cool water. While still wet, neutralize the fabric by immersing it in 1 gallon (3.8 liters) of warm water and ¾ cup (177 ml) of white vinegar. Soak for 10 minutes.

7 Rinse the fabric again in the rinse cycle of the washing machine.

8 Dry fabric and manipulate again in preparation for an additional dyebath or immerse cloth in a new dyebath while still damp.

SUPPLIES

- Respirator
- Heavy gloves, such as the upper-arm-length gloves from PRO Chem
- Fan
- Fabric made from cellulose fiber (cotton, linen, hemp, rayon)
- Thiourea dioxide powder
- Soda ash
- White vinegar
- Measuring spoons
- Measuring cup
- Bucket
- Large enamel or stainless steel pot (dedicated to discharging)
- Wooden spoon or tongs (dedicated to discharging)
- Stove or hot plate
- Rubber bands or string for making bound resists

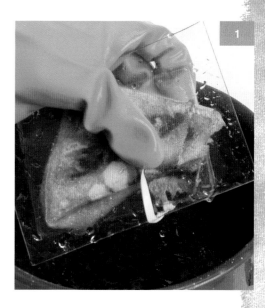

1

SUPPLIES

- Fabric
- *Tools:* Stamps, stencils, Thermofax screens, silkscreens, or brushes
- Thiourea dioxide powder
- Soda ash
- Sodium alginate SH (high viscosity)
- Metaphos water softener
- Blender (dedicated to studio use)
- Spatula
- Measuring spoons
- Measuring cup
- 2 one-gallon (3.8 liter) containers
- 1 quart (946 ml) container
- Old towel
- Steam iron
- Padded surface for printing
- White vinegar

This recipe can be used on cellulose or protein fibers; it makes one gallon of thickened paste, which can be kept in the refrigerator. Neutralize protein fibers with white vinegar after discharge printing is completed, by following the directions on page 83.

discharging by printing with thiox on natural fiber

1 To mix print paste, fill the blender half full of water from a premeasured gallon (3.8 liters) of hot water. Turn the blender on high and add 3 tablespoons (45 ml) of sodium alginate SH. Blend on high until dissolved.

2 Repeat the above process with more water from the premeasured gallon of water, adding 2 more tablespoons (30 ml) of sodium alginate. Combine all the blended water/sodium alginate solution with any remaining water from the gallon container.

3 Allow the mixture to stand overnight to thicken into a smooth paste. If thicker or thinner print past is desired, adjust the amount of sodium alginate accordingly.

4 To mix the discharge paste, pour thickened sodium alginate paste into the 1-quart (946 ml) container. Add the following ingredients in order:
  - ½ teaspoon (2.5 ml) metaphos or Calgon water softener
  - ½ teaspoon (2.5 ml) thiox
  - ½ teaspoon (2.5 ml) soda ash

5 Stir thoroughly to blend ingredients together **(fig. 1)**. The paste is ready for immediate use. Discard any leftover paste at the end of the printing session.

6 Apply print paste to fabric using stamps, stencils, silkscreens, or handpainting with brushes **(fig. 2)**.

7 Don't wait for the paste to dry before steaming. Use a good steam iron and heat the printed image using a pouncing motion **(fig. 3)**. Never set the iron down on damp paste. Use the heat to dry out the fabric slightly before applying contact heat. Heat to the desired lightness.

8 Dampen an old tea towel and fold it in half. Put it next to the iron on the ironing board or worktable. Use it to wipe off the bottom of the iron as you work. The damp terry cloth "scrubs" the iron and keeps the thiox paste from sticking and burning to the bottom of the iron **(fig. 4)**.

9 To stabilize the fabric, rinse it thoroughly in cool water. For protein-based fibers, while still wet, neutralize the fabric by immersing it in 1 gallon (3.8 liters) of warm water and ¾ cup (177 ml) of white vinegar. Soak for 10 minutes and rinse again.

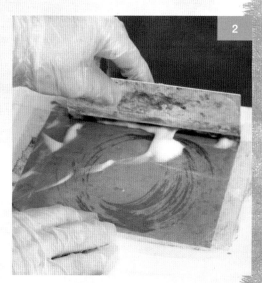

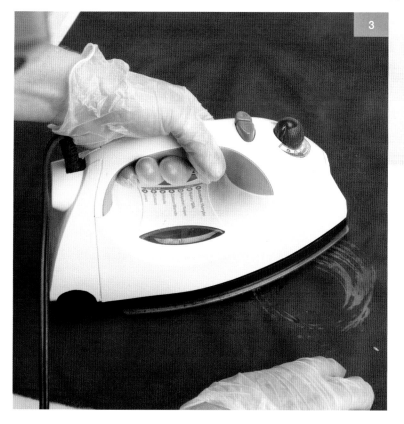

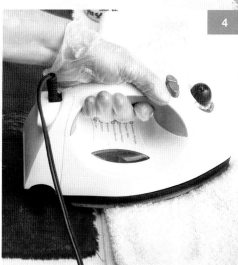

PROCESS:
ADDING DISCHARGE SAMPLES TO THE DYE NOTEBOOK

- Dyed fabric samples or supplies for immersion dyeing, as described on page 46
- Discharge agent(s) of choice:
- Chlorine bleach
- Thickened bleach product: Soft Scrub, Comet Gel, etc.
- Thiourea dioxide
- Rit Color Remover
- Jacquard Discharge Paste
- Respirator
- Rubber gloves
- Fan
- Small containers for thickened products
- *Tools:* Brushes, stencils, stamps, Thermofax screens, silkscreens other than photo-emulsion screens
- Large ceramic or stainless steel pot if preparing a hot-immersion solution (dedicated to discharging)
- Wooden tongs (dedicated to discharging)
- Stove or hot plate
- Water
- Copy paper
- Glue stick
- Notebook
- Hole punch

If you assembled the Dye Notebook as instructed in Chapter 3, add to it by sampling discharged color on your dyed fabric samples. Make samples for any discharge agent you intend to use regularly.

adding discharge samples to the dye notebook

1 Cut dyed and washed fabric into strips. If four agents are tested—bleach, thiourea dioxide (thiox), Jacquard Discharge Paste, and Rit Color Remover, for example—cut fabric squares into four equal strips. If fewer agents are tested, fewer strips are needed. If a thickened bleach product is included in the testing, make sample strips for it also, as the thickened bleach products produce color changes different from straight bleach.

2 Apply discharging agents to each of the sets of strips. Work on one set of strips, with one discharging agent at a time. Remember not to use bleach on a protein fiber. If silk is tested, use the Rit Color Remover, Jacquard Discharge Paste, and the thiox, but eliminate the bleach. Cotton, rayon, and other cellulose fibers are appropriately discharged with all of the agents.

3 Add washed and stabilized samples to your notebook. This resource allows you to check discharged color at a glance, on a variety of fabric types, and can be invaluable in your work with layering processes.

Discharge samples in the notebook.

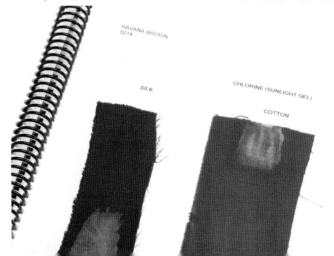

HAVANA BROWN
5214

SILK

CHLORINE (SUNLIGHT GEL)

COTTON

TROUBLESHOOTING DISCHARGE PROCESSES

Discharging color from dyed fabrics is both science and art. As you experiment, you'll learn more about how each discharge agent behaves on various fabrics, and you'll gain proficiency in achieving targeted results instead of random occurrences. Here are some areas for inquiry if you run into problems.

fabric develops holes or other damage

❖ Was the discharge solution too strong?

❖ Was the fabric immersed or treated for too long? Monitor the timing closely.

fabric fails to change color during the discharge application

❖ Was the chosen discharge agent compatible with the fabric? You may have problems with commercial fabric dyed with an incompatible dye or those treated with a resistant finish. Some fiber-reactive MX dyes also resist discharging, including turquoise and fuchsia. Making a comprehensive dye notebook alerts you to these problems in advance.

❖ Was the discharge agent too old, watered down, or exhausted? Try fresh chemicals if necessary.

Apply discharge agents to fabrics to preview the color that will result at the end of the process.

making tools:
stamps and stencils

Stamping and stenciling are two popular ways of making marks on fabric. Though these processes are simple enough for children to enjoy, they also offer infinite possibilities for sophisticated and beautiful art cloth. **Stamping** is a mark made by pressing a tool coated with wet medium (paint, dye paste, discharge paste, or adhesive) onto cloth. A **stencil** is a flat template with open cutouts. You can purchase stencils or make them from plastic, stiff card stock, or appropriated objects, or use my technique for an interfacing-and-net stencil. Whenever a stencil is employed in the layering process, a wet medium is applied with a brush or roller over the open areas of the stencil, and the design transfers onto the cloth.

Detail, Meditation No. 1, Jane Dunnewold, 2005.
Silk broadcloth with fiber-reactive dyes, Rit Color Remover,
textile paints, Prismacolor pencil, and metal leaf.

STAMPING

Stamps are as simple as appropriated tools—can lids, the side of a Plexiglas block, or implements raided from the kitchen drawer—or as complex as intricately carved blocks of wood or soft plastic. A potato masher inked with paint is an appropriated stamping tool. An eraser carved with a pattern is one of the best stamps around. Coiled twine glued to a Plexiglas block is one more version of a stamp. The possibilities are endless!

Stamps are accessible and immediate, so making and collecting them is a perfect way to begin building your toolbox. Making stamps gives you a set of tools capable of printing dye or paint, discharge agent, or adhesive for foiling and metal leaf. Clean your stamps religiously and they will last forever.

MAKING YOUR OWN STAMPS

Although you can use appropriated tools to make some great fabric, take the plunge and learn to cut a stamp yourself. Practice cutting with an X-Acto knife or linoleum-cutting tool until it feels natural in your hand and don't be afraid to make a mistake. I advise cutting a number of stamps in one sitting, because stream of consciousness kicks in, and the stamps exhibit a theme or similarity that ties them together visually.

White plastic erasers (sometimes called soap erasers) are ideal for your first stamps; they're small, easy to cut, and inexpensive, so you can cut lots of stamps and not be too disappointed if you decide to throw one out. A carefully executed stamp made from a white plastic eraser will last for years. Avoid beige gum erasers, as the gum disintegrates easily, and classic rubber erasers with slanted sides, which are dense and difficult to cut.

A variety of cutting tools are available. I prefer an X-Acto knife with a #11 blade. The knife is as sleek as a pencil and easy to hold, so my hand doesn't tire as it might with a thicker barrel. The blade is thin and sharp; in addition to cutting accurately, it serves to remove bits of eraser from the completed stamp. Some artists prefer tools designed to cut linoleum blocks, a set of curved, beveled, and straight cutters that fit into a universal handle. A former student, a gynecologist, preferred a tiny scalpel, and if her stamp cutting was any indication, she was a master surgeon.

Once you have carved several small stamps, graduate to a larger surface. Speedball makes a print block larger than a standard eraser but just as easy to cut. Many art supply stores and online resources sell stamping bases, including eraser-like blocks of plastic and sandblasting stencils that were originally designed to apply text to monuments and gravestones.

Stamps and stamp-making tools.

Why Make Your Own Stamps, Stencils, and Silkscreens?

Why not use commercial stamps, stencils or silkscreen images instead of making your own? It's a question worth considering. Lots of neat-looking tools fill the shelves of hobby and craft stores everywhere. Here are the reasons I want you to make your own tools:

❖ **Cost.** Making tools is less expensive than buying the tools sold in a store.

❖ **Copyright issues.** Most commercial tools come with a disclaimer. They are for personal use only and can't be sold as part of a finished work of art. Even if you might never get caught or face prosecution, it's unethical to pass someone else's designs off as your own. And you can probably design better stuff anyway!

❖ **Filling the toolbox.** It's a good thing to know how to make tools. If you know exactly what look you need for the piece currently in production, your work will benefit by being integrated and cohesive.

❖ **Refinement.** Making tools allows you to generate a repertoire of images that actually support one another thematically. Creating a stable of elements that relate to each other refines your work and is also a key to working in a series.

❖ **Scale.** Commercial stamps designed for use on paper are not good candidates for fabric printing. The delicate nature of the images isn't usually the right scale for printing on cloth. Bigger commercial stamps don't always have enough detail. Be inspired by stamps meant for paper but translate them into your own designs, so that the scale and refinement supports your artistic vision.

PROCESS:
MAKING STAMPS WITH ERASERS

SUPPLIES

- Pencil or pen
- Black inkpad and paper
- 4 to 6 white plastic erasers
- #11 X-Acto knife
- Cutting mat
- Emery board or fine-gauge sandpaper
- E6000 glue to adhere erasers to Plexiglas
- Plexiglas, clear, 4" x 6" (10 x 15 cm) or other sizes as needed for stamps

Additional optional supplies for stamp making:

larger plastic print blocks, sheets of sandblasting stencil, linoleum-cutting tools, hot-melt glue gun

Remember that the image on a stamp will be reversed when it is printed; if you are cutting an alphabet, you must cut the letters backward. The idea of positive and negative space is important. If the design being cut is recessed into the eraser, the print will always be a printed rectangle with an open interior design. If you intend to cut a shape that will print as a positive image, draw it on the eraser and then cut away the excess around it. Making a few mistakes may be the best way to get these qualities figured out.

making stamps with erasers

1 Always work on a flat surface. Use a cutting mat to protect the table. Never hold the eraser in your hand as you cut!

2 If desired, draw a design on the eraser before you begin cutting. This isn't always necessary; sometimes it's fun to cut without having a clear idea of what you are creating, but drawing the shape you intend to cut helps get the scale right for the size of the eraser.

3 If you are using an X-Acto knife, make the first cut straight up and down. Cut down into the eraser at least one-third of its thickness **(fig. 1)**. Shallow cuts fill up with whatever printing medium you're using, resulting in messy prints.

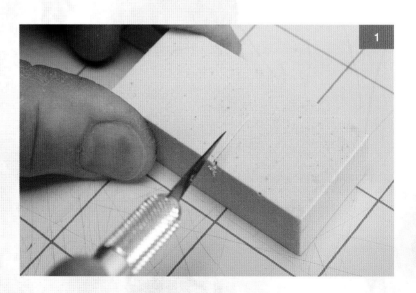

4 Make the second cut at an angle into the first cut. Picture the first cut as a wall. The second cut should cut to the wall, but not through it, which would weaken the underlying structure of the stamp. Cut carefully so that a firm base is preserved, otherwise the stamp will easily break apart **(fig. 2 and fig. 3)**.

5 Cut curves with the wall image in mind. The first cut should be straight up and down. Use the point of the knife to make the curved first cut. Then angle the knife so that the second cut leans into the "wall." Cut up to it, never through it **(fig. 4)**.

6 Use the tip of the knife to cut round elements or squares into the rectangular surface. Remember that it doesn't matter what the eraser looks like below the printing surface. Dig out excess eraser any way that works for you, as long as the printing surface is uniform. Use the stamp pad to check your progress. Printing the image indicates where more eraser could be removed or where an edge needs to be cleaned up.

7 If a piece of the stamp is accidentally cut away, repair it with E6000 glue. Stick a straight pin through from the back to hold the repair in place until the glue dries.

8 To attach the cut stamp to a Plexiglas base, sand the bottom of the eraser with the emery board or fine-gauge sandpaper to rough up the surface. Use E6000 or a glue gun to attach the stamp to the Plexiglas and weight the stamp to keep it aligned while the glue dries.

9 If desired, glue two or more erasers together on Plexiglas to make a larger printing block **(fig. 5)**.

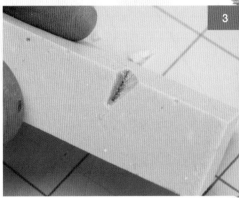

MORE STAMP-MAKING OPTIONS

Try these additional ideas for working with eraser stamps and other stamp-making materials.

❖ Acquire a linoleum cutting set and practice cutting stamps. Some people find these tools easier to use, especially on curves. Keep in mind the importance of making deep cuts, so the lines won't fill up quickly with medium during printing **(fig. 1 and 2)**.

❖ Cut sandblasting stencil material with an X-Acto knife or scissors. Cut two thicknesses as one, so that the final stamp won't be too shallow to use with thicker mediums.

❖ Attach individual pieces of hook-and-loop tape to the back of each eraser stamp and then attach long strips of the partnering tape to a large piece of Plexiglas. The hook-and-loop tape allows you to mix and match stamps, changing the pattern every time fabric is printed, or aiding multiple or production prints. A former student, Shelly Kyle, perfected this approach and printed entire scarf lengths with one large Plexiglas printing "plate."

❖ Add handles to stamps with hook-and-loop tape. Buy two or three wooden knobs at the home supply and position the hook portion of the hook-and-loop tape on each knob base. Attach opposite half of the fastener to individual stamps **(fig. 3)**. Choose the stamp intended for printing and add the temporary handle to ease the printing process.

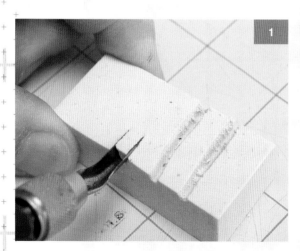

❖Foam rubber (available at upholstery shops in several thicknesses) is too resilient to cut easily with a knife, but it's ideal for patterning with a wood or stencil-burning tool. With this method, you can create a delicate, fine line with the tip of the burner. Any intricate design that can be traced onto the foam can be created with the stencil burner and a healthy dose of patience. Remember that you are melting a synthetic product, so always wear a respirator with appropriate cartridges or work outdoors.

❖Appropriated tools are all around us. Some of my favorites, developed by students in my workshops:
- Bubble wrap
- Potato masher
- Kitchen scrub pad
- Weather stripping tape on Plexiglas (it already has adhesive on it)
- Keys
- Styrofoam meat trays (incise these with a pencil or other blunt instrument)
- Plastic lace tablemats
- Twine or rope glued to Plexiglas with a hot glue gun.

3

PRINTING WITH STAMPS

Stamping always involves coating an object—created or appropriated—with wet medium, followed by pressing it onto the base cloth. If too much paint, discharge paste, or anything else wet is applied to the stamp, it will squish out along the edges and blur the print.

When you apply any product to the stamp, therefore, be conservative; it doesn't take much paint, dye, or glue to make a clean and consistent print. Use a foam brush to apply wet medium, unless you want brush strokes on the stamp to be a design element. If the stamp is small, use a small brush to apply the wet medium. If the stamp is large, use a bigger brush or a small foam roller **(fig. 1)**. Scaling tools to be the same approximate size ensures clean printing.

While the brush application provides more control over printing than dipping the stamp into a tray of paint or bleach, another option is to make a stamp pad large enough to accommodate your stamp. Use two layers of felt, saturated with paint, bleach, dye, or adhesive, in a Styrofoam tray.

Be rigorous in cleaning stamps when you are finished printing with them. Use an old toothbrush and cool water to clean stamps thoroughly **(fig. 2)**. No soap is required. Let the stamps dry completely before you put them away, to avoid mold and mildew. Store stamps in a covered container to keep them dust-free.

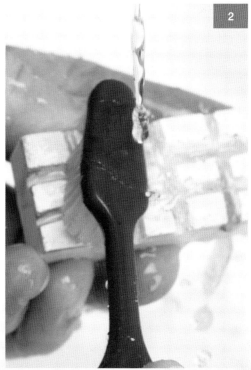

TROUBLESHOOTING STAMPING PROBLEMS

stamp prints illegibly

❖ Did you apply too much wet medium prior to stamping?

❖ Does your stamp have cut-away areas that are too shallow? If so, deepen the grooves with an X-Acto knife.

stamps break or parts split off

❖ Did you take care while carving the stamp to ensure a stable base? If the block is large, such as a Speedball printing block, stabilize it by gluing to a Plexiglas base. If needed, repair the stamp with E6000 adhesive.

stamps glued to a plexiglas backing pop off or don't adhere

❖ Did you sand the back of each stamp with an emery board or sandpaper to rough up the surface before gluing it to a base?

❖ Did you use an appropriate flexible permanent glue, such as E6000 or a hot-melt glue gun?

stamps appear to be clogged or no longer print cleanly after several uses

❖ Did you allow paint to dry on the stamp? If so, it cannot be removed.

❖ Did you allow other wet media to dry on the stamp? If so, try removing with hot water and a stiff toothbrush.

The stamp on the left was clogged with paint and allowed to dry before it was cleaned. The stamp in the middle broke during printing; the original cuts were not carefully executed. The stamp on the right prints illegibly because the cuts aren't deep enough.

STENCILING

Stencils have a long and diverse history, dating back to Paleolithic cave paintings completed between 30000 and 9000 B.C. Fiji Islanders cut holes in banana leaves and stenciled through the cutouts, and Eskimo peoples used dried sealskin as a stencil material. Today, stencils are an infinitely versatile tool for adding print and pattern to art cloth.

Art cloth by Leslie Morgan.

CREATING YOUR OWN STENCILS

Stencils are easy to cut and long-lasting, making it possible to print an image many times and to use a host of processes, including dyes, discharge agents, textile paints, resists, and adhesives. Commercial stencils are available in craft stores and online; plastic and highly durable, the potential downside of purchasing a commercial stencil is the copyright issue—consider whether or not the image can be used legally on artwork you might sell. Commercial stencils also introduce limitations of image size, scale, and style.

It's easy, however, to make your own stencils from your own designs. Cut stencils from card stock, cardboard, thin plastic, or clear transparency film. If the design is complicated, make the stencil permanent by choosing a waterproof foundation instead of cardboard or paper. On the other hand, if the stencil is a one-time proposition, freezer paper is a terrific choice since it can be ironed directly onto the cloth and removed when stenciling is completed.

Materials for stencil making and stenciling.

design considerations for making stencils

You'll find inspiration for stencil designs from a wide range of sources. Sketch a design before actually cutting it. Drawing a sample will help you figure out two logistical considerations. It's important to know which parts of the design will be the positive, or the figure, and which parts of the design will be negative space, or background, as you make decisions about what to cut away and what to leave behind.

You must also consider how detailed the stencil should be. An effective stencil can be a simplified version of the image that inspired it, but with a bit more time and patience, it can just as easily be an intricate or complex version of the image. For example, one stencil of a bird could be made with the key parts—wing, body, tail, and beak—cut out of the background as individual components. In this approach to designing, the viewer's eye puts the parts together and sees the bird. The proximity of the separate parts becomes an important factor. If the individual components of the bird are too far apart on the background, our eyes won't connect them and *see* the bird.

Another way to design the bird is to cut out a single shape that looks like a bird. This version is, in effect, a silhouette of the bird. If you are in doubt about whether your stencil looks enough like the original inspiration to be recognizable, ask someone else what the stencil image looks like. It's the only way to ensure accurate recognition once the artwork is printed.

Explore positive and negative spaces before cutting your stencil to be sure you get the design you want.

A stencil can be cut as a simple, complete shape, or as individual elements that read as one image. Decide in advance of cutting the stencil which variation you prefer.

INTERFACING AS MODERN STENCIL MATERIAL

Detail makes a stencil more visually engaging. A silhouette of a bird may be perfect for one piece of artwork, but another piece might benefit from a bird with detailed elements. The classic method of building detail into a stencil is the inclusion of *bridges*—tiny strips of paper or cardboard left intact as part of the background, to keep the network of detail parts connected. Classic Japanese stencils use thin strands of human hair or silk to hold the sections of a mulberry paper stencil together.

I've always loved observing traditional processes to figure out contemporary approaches to those old techniques. I found the mulberry paper and silk gauze stencils particularly captivating. I knew there had to be a modern way to mimic those stencils.

Enter the midnight brainstorm: fusible interfacing, the contemporary alternative to mulberry paper and silk gauze! Non-woven, fusible polyester interfacing is easy to cut, inexpensive and sold at fabric stores everywhere. Choose interfacing about the weight of a sheet of copy paper. The adhesive should be a continuous coating across the back of the interfacing to ensure that the stencil will fuse securely. Don't buy interfacing with tiny dots of fusible.

Interfacing is a perfect modern stencil material.

PROCESS:
MAKING A STENCIL WITH INTERFACING AND NYLON NET

These stencils are tough and durable and can be used to print any wet product—dye, paint, discharging agents, resists, and adhesives. I've even used mine with spray paint and produced terrific results.

Nylon net or tulle acts as a middle layer in an interfacing stencil, providing a porous, stable surface that allows wet media to penetrate and print. The open net makes it easy to "float" design elements where bridges would have been required in a traditional stencil. The net used for scrubbing pads is slightly thicker than tulle, and the texture usually remains when the stencil is printed. Tulle is more delicate than net, and the fine texture disappears when the pattern is printed. Try both versions of net to compare end results.

making a stencil with interfacing and nylon net

1   Cut two pieces of fusible interfacing the same size. The stencil can be any size, even really big, but start with a manageable size such as 8" x 10" (20.5 x 25.5 cm) **(fig. 1)**. Position the fusible sides face to face together. Do not iron yet.

2   Draw a 1" (2.5 cm) border around the perimeter of the interfacing to remind yourself to stay inside the line.

1

Tulle (left) has smaller openings than nylon net (right).

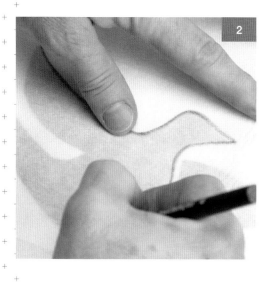

3 Draw a design on the interfacing or trace one from another source **(fig. 2)**. Use the X-Acto knife and cutting mat to cut out the design through both layers at once.

4 Cut a piece of net or tulle big enough to fit inside the sandwich but leave an extension of net on one side to make it easy to hang up while drying **(fig. 3)**.

5 Layer the netting between the interfacing layers, matching the cut pattern exactly **(fig. 4)**.

6 Fuse the layers together following the manufacturer's instructions, starting in the center and work toward the edges with the fusing process. Use parchment paper or a pressing cloth to protect the interfacing from melting **(fig. 5)**.

7 To begin the painting and sealing process, cover the worktable with plastic, as paper will stick to the interfacing when it gets wet. Coat both sides of the interfacing sandwich thoroughly with paint **(fig. 6)**. Don't be concerned about painting over the netting because when the stencil is lifted off the table most of the paint on the netting will stay on the plastic.

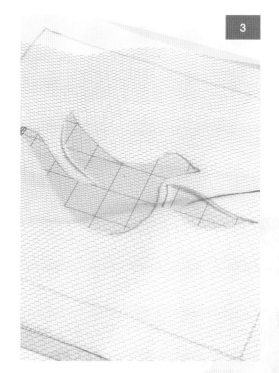

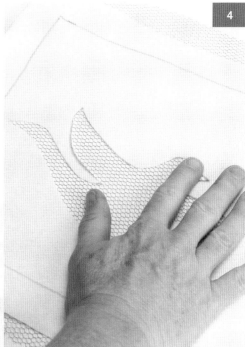

8   Small bits of paint in the net can be a pleasing textural feature, but if you'd rather keep the net surface completely open, remove wet paint with a cotton swab or clean brush. Hold the stencil up to the light to check for pinholes and fill those in with more paint. If free-floating pieces aren't thoroughly stuck, don't worry—these can be ironed again to glue them down when the paint dries or glued in place with fusible web later.

9   Hang the stencil up to dry. Don't dry it flat or it may stick to the plastic. Once dry, trim the stencil to remove the excess net and square it up. Press the stencil front and back to set the paint. Store dry interfacing stencils upright in a file folder to keep them dust-free and flat.

10 Interfacing stencils are washable after the original paint application is set with an iron. After using a stencil to apply wet media to fabric, rinse the stencil in cool water and hang it up to dry. If it warps slightly during the drying process, use a steam iron to flatten it out before you use it again. I use a parchment sheet for protection when I steam stencils flat.

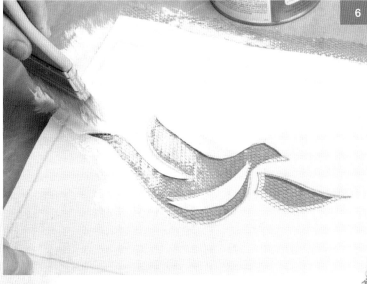

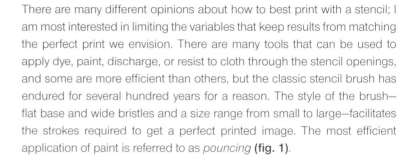

PROCESS:
PRINTING WITH A STENCIL

S U P P L I E S

- Base cloth
- Stencil
- Textile paint or other wet media such as dye paste (page 54), discharge paste (page 84), or adhesive for foiling (page 160)
- Flat plate or piece of Plexiglas to hold paint
- Stencil brush (if you're using a chlorine bleach product, choose a brush with synthetic fiber bristles)
- Scrap paper

There are many different opinions about how to best print with a stencil; I am most interested in limiting the variables that keep results from matching the perfect print we envision. There are many tools that can be used to apply dye, paint, discharge, or resist to cloth through the stencil openings, and some are more efficient than others, but the classic stencil brush has endured for several hundred years for a reason. The style of the brush—flat base and wide bristles and a size range from small to large—facilitates the strokes required to get a perfect printed image. The most efficient application of paint is referred to as *pouncing* **(fig. 1)**.

printing with a stencil

1 Position the stencil on the base fabric in the desired location and steady it with your free hand. Don't pin it in place, as you will be moving it several times.

2 Pour a small amount of wet medium (dye, paint, discharge paste, etc.) onto a flat plate or piece of Plexiglas.

3 Tamp the stencil brush into the wet medium on the palette.

4 Distribute paint evenly by pouncing (an up and down motion with the brush) on a piece of scrap paper or the tray where the wet medium is located. When the wet medium is evenly distributed on the brush, move to the stencil that you have positioned on the fabric.

5 Pounce the wet medium onto the cloth, using steady, rhythmic motions **(fig. 1)**. Don't overdo it. This is a gradual process of adding color, discharge, resist, or adhesive to the cloth.

6 Lift the corner of the stencil to check progress. Don't pull the whole thing away! Lift a corner gently, so you can ascertain where more wet media or color should be added **(fig. 2)**.

7 Once stenciling is completed, wash the stencil and hang it to dry. Store the stencil in a file folder or punch a hole in the border corner so that it can be hung from a cup hook in the studio.

OTHER STENCIL IDEAS

TROUBLESHOOTING STENCIL PROBLEMS

The interfacing stencil is a long-lasting, sturdy tool if cared for properly. But sometimes the right tool has an immediate "there you are and I am grabbing you" momentum. This requires on-the-spot acknowledgment and acquisition. For example:

* **Any flat surface** with cutouts can be appropriated as a stencil—sequin waste, paper leaves from the florist, weird trash from the street.

* **Leaves from a flower or other plant.** Stenciling isn't only what's *inside* the shape. Sometimes pouncing over the outside border of a leaf or paper or other odd this or that is exactly the right treatment.

* **Freezer paper.** What a glorious invention this is! Buy it in rolls at the grocery store. It can be cut with scissors, adheres temporarily to fabric and can then be peeled away as soon as a wet application is completed, and even rinses so that it can be used more than once. Finished? Pitch it into the paper recycling bin. Perhaps you'll live long enough to encounter it again later in some reincarnate form. We should all be so lucky.

Interesting shapes result from stenciling outside a shape.

When printing discharge paste, use less wet medium than would be true of paint or dye. Review Chapter 4 for information on using discharge processes. Because wet discharge paste will be ironed, it's important to deposit less paste on the fabric, so the excess won't clump and then smear while heating, ruining the clarity of the image. Tips for other stencil printing problems:

interfacing doesn't stick after heating

* Was the iron hot enough?
* Did you allow enough time to elapse while the heat was applied?
* Did you just miss a section? Try reheating the interfacing; if that doesn't work, put a tiny piece of fusible web between the layers of interfacing and heat the whole thing again.

paint doesn't cover completely
(or there are small holes that let wet media through while printing)

* Are you using enough paint? Give the stencil another application. Sometimes paint is too thin, sometimes we are too polite in the application! Paint can always be added to fill small pinholes.

edges of the print blur and are never really clear

* Did you apply the wet media properly? Pounce the stencil brush up and down.
* Did you use the right brush?
* Did you pounce first on scrap paper and then move on to the cloth? Work for clean edges and just the right amount of wet medium to make a print that reveals all detail and keeps a clear outline.

print and pattern:
water-based resists

We considered one method of generating a resist when, in advance of dyeing, cloth is bound with rubber bands or string (page 48). This chapter explores a second version of resist—the application of a water-based product to the cloth, which dries and temporarily blocks access to the fabric surface, to add pattern and contrast. Dye or paint applied over a resist flows around it but can't flow into or under it. Once the paint or dye dries and is stabilized, the resist is washed out, revealing the patterning. Water-based resists are especially valuable to those artists who prefer not to use discharging agents due to health and safety concerns, as the resists mimic the look of discharging without exposure to the chemicals.

Types of Water-based Resists :: Soy Wax as a Resist :: Water-soluble Glue as a Resist :: Flour Paste as a Resist :: Combining Resist and Discharge Processes Resists and Color :: Troubleshooting

Detail, Archetype Series: Guide II, Jane Dunnewold, 2007.
Silk broadcloth with flour-paste resist, mixed dye color split into red and green, textile paints, permanent marker, needlefelting.

An effective resist must meet two criteria. First, the resist must be thin enough to penetrate the threads of the selected fabric. If the resist can't seep into the threads and temporarily block them from receiving the dye or discharge medium, it will fail. Second, the resist must be water-soluble and removable after the dye, paint, or discharge agent dries and sets, or is ready for wash out. A water-based resist means that the resist goes onto the cloth wet but washes out after the colorant is applied and stabilized. Don't confuse water-based resists with *gutta*, a solvent-based resist employed during traditional dye painting. Gutta is different from the resists discussed here, as it is removed by dry-cleaning or is left permanently in the fabric as a design element.

The above criteria apply to any product intended for use as a resist on fabric. Dye suppliers sell commercial water-based resists, but my testing indicated unreliable performance. I prefer to focus on three readily available and effective water-based resists because of their reliability and versatility.

Soy wax is a soybean derivative. Unlike microcrystalline wax, petroleum-based paraffin wax, or beeswax, soy wax washes out of fabric with detergent and hot water. It doesn't reconstitute as it cools; rather, it dissolves, allowing disposal without risk of damage to plumbing. Soy is a nontoxic, renewable, and versatile resource. It can be stamped or stenciled, or fabric can be dipped into it, mimicking bound-resist patterning.

Water-soluble glue, such as Elmer's Glue, is inexpensive and nontoxic. This glue washes out of clothing easily and without staining since it's designed with children in mind. Create pattern by directly applying the glue straight from the bottle or by stamping, screening, or stenciling.

Flour paste is as versatile as glue and almost foolproof. Apply ordinary white flour mixed with water to the surface of the cloth with a brush or squeegee. Hairline cracks and crevices are characteristic visual qualities of a flour-paste resist.

Water-based resist materials.

Soy-wax granules can be melted for use as a resist.

SOY WAX AS A RESIST

Soy wax revolutionizes the use of wax resist. Soy cools more slowly than other wax, making it a great candidate for stamping, stenciling, and folded and dipped applications. Since soy wax washes out in hot water, it eliminates the need for ironing or dry cleaning, the preferred methods for removal of beeswax or paraffin. Soy wax's environmentally friendly and nontoxic nature counts in laundry rooms, kitchens, and studios. The wax won't hurt septic systems or pipes, and it's biodegradable.

Several grades of soy wax are available from manufacturers, local merchants, and online venues. Wax meant for use on cloth is sold in pellet or granule form. Be sure to purchase wax from a reliable source (see Resources, page 173). Don't scrimp; price is usually an indication of quality. Lower grade (less expensive) soy wax is harder to wash out and could potentially damage a washing machine or plumbing. If in doubt as to quality, buy a small amount of wax first, try it, and then buy a larger quantity if it works well.

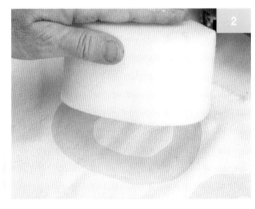

You'll find that soy wax is extremely versatile. Methods of successful application for soy wax include:

❖ Manipulate fabric as for immersion dyeing (folding, pleating, tying rings, etc). Dip edges in hot wax. Set the waxed piece aside to cool **(fig. 1)**. I use the freezer to speed cooling of the wax. Place waxed bundles on a piece of Plexiglas reserved for this purpose and put the Plexiglas in the freezer for ten minutes. Once the wax cools, open the fabric and dye it in an immersion dyebath.

❖ Tape fabric to the tabletop. Wax the fabric on a non-absorbent surface such as melamine or stainless steel **(fig. 2)**. Scrape the wax that penetrates through the cloth off the printing surface with a squeegee or similar tool and return it to the pot. Spread wax across the surface with a brush or roll hot wax onto the cloth with a roller. Try textures underneath the fabric. I use an old roll-down window shade under the cloth. Allow the wax to cool and then dye by immersing or handpainting with dye.

❖ Apply hot wax with a stencil brush or bristle brush **(fig. 3)**. Dedicate tools to stenciling with wax, as it is difficult to reclaim waxed tools.

❖ Wax with appropriated tools. Stamp wax with a round lid, or other nontraditional object. A potato masher is one of my favorites. Allow wax to cool before applying dye.

PROCESS:
COMBINING SOY WAX AND FIBER-REACTIVE DYE

There's no limit to what you can do with this combination of resist method and coloring agent. Try several different fabrics at the start so you can begin to learn the way each fabric behaves with these materials.

combining soy wax and fiber-reactive dye

1   Heat the soy wax in a skillet or double boiler reserved for waxing. Even though the wax is nontoxic, keep food and studio equipment separate. Fill the container about half full to start. Never mix soy wax with other waxes.

2   Apply wax to fabric using one of the application methods described on page 110. Follow with immersion dyeing as described on page 46.

3   No matter which application method you choose, allow fabric to batch overnight before proceeding with the wash out. It isn't necessary to cover fabric with plastic.

4   **Washing machine wax removal method:** Choose a hot wash/warm rinse setting on the washing machine. Water must be 140°F (60°C) or hotter during the first hot cycle. Use a thermometer to gauge water temperature the first time you use the washer. Sometimes it helps to turn up the thermostat on the hot water heater, but be careful if you are in a home environment. Another way to raise the water temperature is to boil a pot of water on the stove and add it to the washing machine during the first cycle.

5   Add 1 teaspoon (5 ml) of Synthrapol as the washing machine is filling.

6   Complete the entire wash/rinse cycle. Remove the fabric from the washer. If it still feels a little stiff, repeat the hot water/warm rinse cycle a second time.

SUPPLIES

- Fabric
- Soy wax granules
- Electric skillet or hot plate and double boiler for melting wax
- Fiber-reactive MX dyes
- Large enamel or stainless steel pot
- Synthrapol
- *For stamping, stenciling, or handpainting:* Sponge stamps, interfacing stencils, appropriate dedicated brushes, including a stencil brush and a bristle brush 1" (2.5 cm) wide
- *For bound resist:* Rubber bands and string, Plexiglas for use as a cooling rack
- *For tabletop application:* Printing surface (preferably melamine or stainless steel), blue painter's tape, squeegee, optional textures under fabric
- *For immersion dyeing:* Bucket, salt, and soda ash

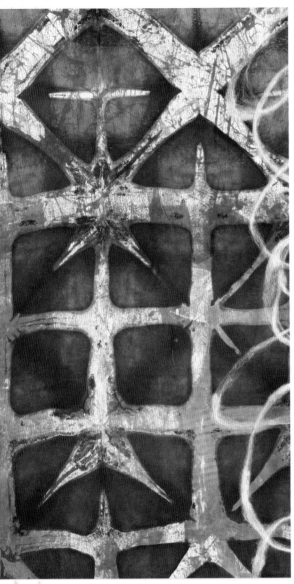

Art cloth made with soy-wax resist and dye.

7 When wax is fully removed, the fabric is ready for a new layer or application of color.

8 **Stovetop wax removal method:** Heavier fabrics such as silk noil and cotton broadcloth retain wax and may require additional processing to facilitate thorough removal. Use a hot plate and large pot if the washing machine method didn't do the trick. Choose a pot large enough to hold the fabric you intend to simmer. Put the cloth in the pot and then fill it with enough water to submerge the fabric.

9 Add 1 teaspoon (5 ml) Synthrapol to the pot. Bring the water to a low simmer.

10 Stir the fabric in the hot water until the wax is dissolved. Wax floats to the top of the kettle and looks like scum when it dissolves. Keep the water at a low simmer.

11 When the wax is fully removed, the fabric is ready for a new layer or application of color.

Fabric stamped with wax and ready to dye.

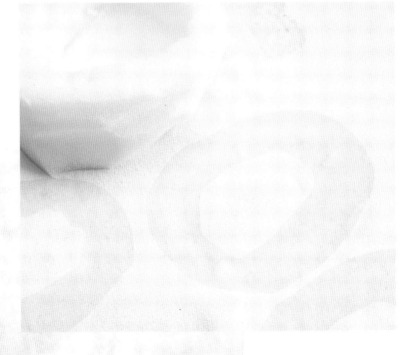

PROCESS:
COMBINING SOY WAX AND TEXTILE PAINT

Substitute watercolor-weight textile paint, such as Dye-Na-Flow, Setasilk, or Deka Silk Paint, for dye in the previous instructions. Once again, experiment with several different fabrics to discover how the wax and paint combination behaves on each one. Two important factors for consideration:

1   Thin paint works better than thick paint because the fabric stays softer and more flexible. Too heavy an application of paint complicates wax removal. Choose one of the textile paints meant to mimic dye or add a little water to the paint to thin it slightly.

2   Paints usually require heat setting, which is obviously at odds with waxing. Since ironing fabric isn't an option, give the paint several days to set. The longer the paint sets, the better the color. Washing the fabric without providing enough time for air curing may affect the depth of color of the paint.

Layer wax and textile paints numerous times to build a complex visual surface.

Art cloth made with soy-wax resist and textile paints.

WATER-SOLUBLE GLUE AS A RESIST

Washable glue can be used with stamps, stencils, screenprinting, or handpainting techniques. Don't thin the glue with water. It must penetrate the fabric to be effective, so the weave and weight of the cloth are important. Water-soluble glue is well-suited to printing, but immersing a glue-resisted fabric in a dyebath can backfire. The glue may dissolve, depending on the amount of time the cloth is immersed.

Water-soluble glue makes an effective and versatile resist.

PROCESS:
COMBINING WATER-SOLUBLE GLUE AND FIBER-REACTIVE DYE

Buy washable glue, frequently referred to as "school glue." Check the label for washability; it *must* wash out! Elmer's Blue School Gel is a good choice. In some cases, glue bonds permanently to the sizing in unwashed fabric, so always prewash fabric.

combining water-soluble glue and fiber-reactive dye

1 Pin dry fabric to the padded table with T-pins. Iron if needed.

2 Apply the glue to the fabric using stamps, stencil, silkscreen, or a Thermofax screen. Glue can also be handpainted onto the cloth with a brush. Check penetration by turning the edge of the cloth to the back. Glue on the back of the fabric is an indication that it is satisfactorily penetrating the cloth.

3 Allow the glue to dry completely (usually overnight) **(fig 1)**. The surface must be entirely dry to the touch.

4 Apply dye to the fabric. As mentioned above, immersion dyeing is problematic. To be on the safe side, apply dye mixed with print paste with a brush or squeegee to the fabric surface. Add soda ash fixative to print paste as discussed on page 53.

5 Allow dye to batch overnight before removing the glue. Don't cover the fabric with plastic during the batching time, as the moisture dissolves the glue. Allow the fabric to air-dry, resting on the printing surface, or hang the fabric on an indoor clothesline.

6 Remove the resist by washing fabric in cool water in the washing machine. No detergent is needed. One cycle should remove the glue resist, but if it can still be felt in the cloth after washing, launder the cloth a second time.

7 When the glue is removed, the fabric is ready for additional layering or coloration.

SUPPLIES

- Fabric
- T-pins
- Padded surface for printing
- Water-soluble glue, such as Elmer's Blue School Gel
- *Tools:* stamps, stencils, silkscreens, Thermofax screens, or brushes
- Squeegee suited to printing method
- A selection of fiber-reactive MX dyes
- Print paste
- Soda ash fixative (50/50 mix of baking soda and soda ash; see page 53)
- Synthrapol detergent
- Iron

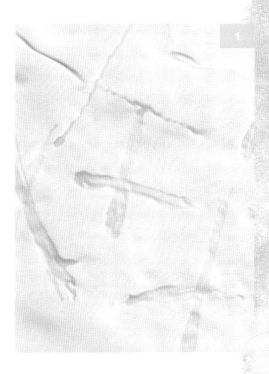

PROCESS:
COMBINING WATER-SOLUBLE GLUE AND TEXTILE PAINT

Just as with other methods, experiment with a variety of different fabrics. I like to use watercolor-weight textile paints for this combination. Heat-set the paints with care and protect your iron with a piece of parchment paper if needed.

combining water-soluble glue and textile paint

1 Pin dry fabric to the padded table with T-pins. Iron if needed.

2 Apply glue to the fabric using stamps, stencil, silkscreen, or a Thermofax screen; glue can also be handpainted onto the cloth with a brush. Check penetration by turning the edge of the cloth to the back. Glue on the back of the fabric is an indication that it is satisfactorily penetrating the cloth.

3 Allow the glue to dry completely (usually overnight). The surface must be entirely dry to the touch.

4 Apply textile paint to the fabric surface with a brush or squeegee.

5 Paints require heat setting **(fig. 1)**. Do this prior to washing out the glue. Iron on the reverse of the fabric or use a piece of parchment paper over the glue to protect the iron.

6 Wash the fabric in cool water in the washing machine. No detergent is needed. One cycle should remove the glue resist, but if it can still be felt in the cloth after washing, launder the cloth a second time.

7 When the glue is removed, the fabric is ready for additional layering or coloration.

Water-based glue is a great way to build layers; be sure the glue dries before the dye or paint is applied to the surface.

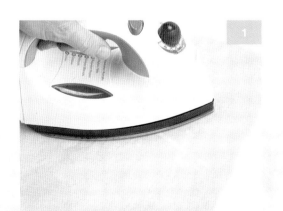

FLOUR PASTE AS A RESIST

Flour paste is nontoxic, inexpensive, and effective as a resist. Apply flour paste to any fabric. It isn't finicky and works as well on synthetics as it does on natural fibers. Consider making several samples, varying the paste thickness and using a variety of fabrics. Compare results once the process is complete, for future reference.

Ordinary inexpensive white flour is the best choice for resist. The large particles in whole wheat flour preclude a smooth paste. I've tried rice flour, cornstarch, and a host of thickeners from Asian markets, and none of them work as well as ordinary white flour. Before I discovered flour paste, I recommended instant mashed potato mixes, but flour paste is a more effective resist.

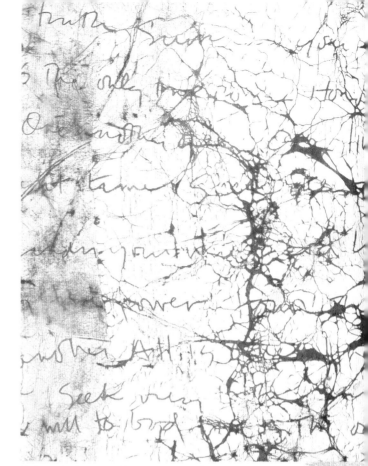

A glue resist is compatible with a previous flour-paste resist; be sure to stabilize each layer.

basic flour-paste recipe

Mix one cup of white flour with one cup of cold water. Add water gradually until the mixture has the consistency of pancake batter **(fig. 1)**. If the paste is too thin, add a bit more flour. If it is too thick, add a bit more water. Don't use hot water or the paste will be gluey. Use a whisk or large spoon to stir the paste until the lumps are gone.

PROCESS:
COMBINING FLOUR-PASTE RESIST AND FIBER-REACTIVE DYE

SUPPLIES

- Fabric
- White flour
- Bowl
- Cold water
- Measuring cup
- Wooden spoon
- T-pins
- Padded printing surface
- Squeegee or wide brush
- Skewer
- A selection of fiber-reactive MX Dyes
- Print paste (see page 54) and soda ash

This process covers the entire cloth with resist, allowing you to draw into the wet surface with tools or simply make an allover textured surface. The flour paste doesn't keep overnight, so don't make more than can be used in one studio session. Make samples with a variety of fabrics.

combining flour-paste resist and fiber-reactive dye

1   Make Basic Flour Paste Recipe (page 117).

2   With T-pins, pin one edge of the fabric to your padded printing surface. Fabric shrinks and curls as the paste dries, and pinning helps keep the cloth flat. However, fabric stretches as the wet paste is pulled across the surface, so wait to pin the other edges until the resist application is completed.

3   Pour flour paste across the pinned edge of the fabric. The amount of flour paste varies depending on the size of the fabric. Just guess to get started. It's easy to add more paste if you run out halfway across the cloth.

4   Spread flour paste across the fabric surface with a wide brush or squeegee **(fig. 1)**. Cover the entire surface with an even coating.

5   To achieve a simple crackle texture, allow the paste to dry thoroughly at this stage.

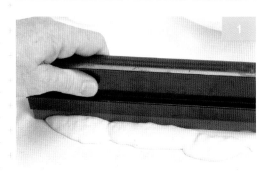

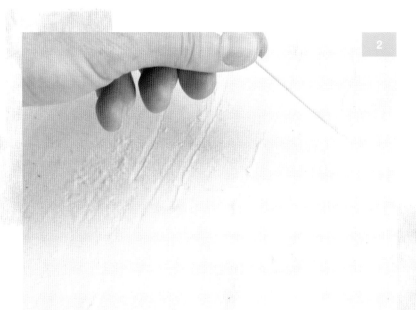

6   If patterning is desired, "draw" into the wet paste with a wooden skewer **(fig. 2)**. Draw patterns, circles, and swirls. I love to write words into the wet paste. "Erase" by smoothing the paste with the squeegee. When you are satisfied with the patterning, pin the three remaining edges of the fabric to the table to keep the fabric flat while it dries.

7   Allow the paste to dry thoroughly—24 hours or more, depending on the humidity. The paste surface will be matte when thoroughly dry.

8   Remove the pins holding the fabric to the printing table.

9   Crackle the fabric by scrunching it. Scrunching fabric too vigorously allows more dye to seep onto the fabric, so don't overdo it.

10 Add soda ash fixative to print paste as described on page 54.

11 Use a wide brush to spread dye paste over the flour-coated surface **(fig. 3)**. If the dye paste is too thick to penetrate the flour paste easily, add a little water to thin it. Work the dye into the paste using pressure, to be sure the dye penetrates it.

12 Allow the dye to batch for 24 hours. Do not cover the fabric with plastic, as the flour paste will soften, compromising its ability to effectively resist the dye.

13 Soak the flour-coated, dye-painted fabric in a bucket of cold water for 10 minutes to dissolve the paste.

14 Pour off the water and put the fabric in a washing machine on a regular cycle. Wash the fabric thoroughly. No additional detergent is required. Heavy cotton or silk noil may require two washes to remove paste completely.

15 Dry the fabric in the dryer and press it with an iron.

16 Once the flour paste is removed, dye the fabric again if desired, consider discharging, or leave it as it is **(fig. 4)**. The potential for drawing, applying more than one color of dye to the surface, and repeated layerings of dye and paste ensure satisfying hours of exploration.

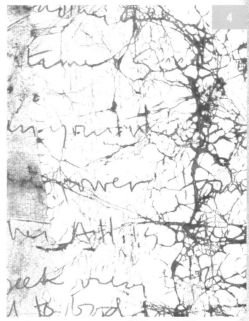

PROCESS:
COMBINING FLOUR-PASTE RESIST AND TEXTILE PAINT

SUPPLIES

- Fabric
- White flour
- Bowl
- Cold water
- Measuring cup
- Wooden spoon
- T-pins
- Padded printing surface
- Squeegee or wide brush
- Watercolor-weight textile paint or thinned acrylic paint
- Bucket
- Cold water
- Washing machine
- Iron

I often use textile paint with flour-paste resist instead of dye. Textile paint doesn't discharge, so if I'm building a surface by alternating layers of dye and discharge, the discharging process doesn't change the crackle texture generated by the paint over flour paste. Using paint over the flour paste generates a permanent texture or pattern that can be covered with one layer of dye and then revealed during the next discharge application— a wonderful means of maximizing the illusion of depth on the surface of the fabric.

combining flour-paste resist and textile paint

1   Follow Steps 1 through 6 on page 118, *Combining Flour-Paste Resist and Fiber-Reactive Dyes.*

2   Remove the pins holding the fabric to the printing table.

3   Crackle the fabric by scrunching it. Scrunching fabric too vigorously allows more paint to seep onto the fabric; so don't overdo it.

4   Thin textile or acrylic paint with water to the consistency of milk or use a thin watercolor-weight textile paint such as Setasilk or Dye-Na-Flow. These paints are already a thin consistency and offer the advantage of maximum pigment load. I use black paint, but any color works.

Below and opposite:
Details of crackled flour-paste and thinned textile paint.

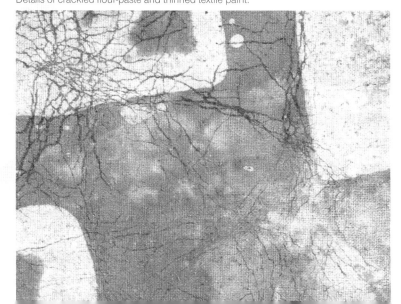

5 Use a wide brush to spread paint over the flour-coated surface. Work the paint into the flour paste using pressure; be sure the paint penetrates the cracks in the paste.

6 Allow the paint to dry.

7 Although textile paint normally requires heat setting, the flour-coated fabric can't be easily ironed, and it is NOT a good idea to put the fabric in the dryer. Instead, wait 24 hours before washing out the fabric. Waiting for as long as a week will not affect the flour paste. It will still wash out. If in doubt, place parchment paper over the painted, flour-coated surface and heat with an iron.

8 To remove the resist, soak the flour-coated, painted fabric in a bucket of cold water for ten minutes to dissolve the paste.

9 Pour off the water and dispose of the flour sludge in the trash. Wash the fabric in a washing machine on regular cycle. No additional soap is required. Heavy cotton or silk noil may require two washes to remove the paste completely.

10 Dry the fabric in the dryer and press with an iron.

11 Once the flour paste is removed, the cloth is ready for additional layers or patterning.

Crackled flour-paste and thinned textile paint comprised the first layer of this art cloth.

COMBINING RESIST AND DISCHARGE PROCESSES

Dyes and paints are not the only option when water-soluble resists are a component in the layering process. Combining resists with discharging processes expands the layering repertoire. Chart your course before beginning actual work on fabric, since resists and discharging agents aren't always compatible with each other. The chart on page 123 shows at a glance which resist and discharge combinations will be successful.

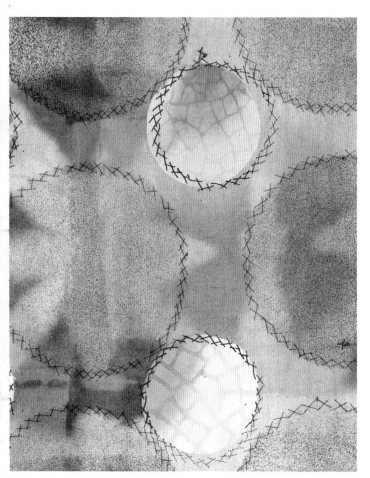

Dyed and discharged circles were cut and fused and "stitches" were screenprinted.

Keep these guidelines in mind:

Fiber content influences the discharging choice. Remember, silk can't be subjected to a chlorine discharge of any kind, while cellulose fibers (cotton, linen, hemp, and rayon) are compatible with all of the discharging agents.

The weight and thickness of the cloth influences the resist choice. For example, no matter what the fiber content, soy wax is a better choice for heavy fabric than glue. Lighter fabrics are more versatile—all three resists (soy wax, water-soluble glue, and flour paste) penetrate thin fabric easily.

A discharge product that requires heat applied with an iron is incompatible with soy wax. Discharge paste and thiox paste are not compatible with soy wax resist.

Some dyes won't discharge. Whether fabric was commercially dyed or hand-dyed, test it to be sure the color can be removed.

Surprisingly enough, soy wax makes a great resist combined with an immersion discharge bath. It withstands a dip in Rit Color Remover or a thiox bath without melting completely, if the wax is hardened and cooled in a freezer prior to discharging.

See Chapter 2, Building Layers, for more ideas on compatible layering of discharge processes and resists.

Resist and Discharge Combinations			
discharge agent	water-based resist: flour paste	water-based resist: glue	water-based resist: soy wax
chlorine bleach (applied liquid)	compatible	compatible	compatible
chlorine bleach (thickened products for printing)	compatible: choose for greater control than liquid chlorine	compatible: choose for greater control than liquid chlorine	compatible: choose for greater control than liquid chlorine
Jacquard Discharge Paste for printing	not compatible: difficult to iron over flour paste	not compatible: ironing over glue poses problems	not compatible: cannot iron over soy wax
Rit Color Remover immersion bath	not compatible	compatible	use caution: compatible, but work quickly
thiourea dioxide (thiox) immersion bath	not compatible	compatible	use caution: compatible, but work quickly
thiourea dioxide (thiox) paste for printing	not compatible: difficult to iron over flour paste	not compatible: ironing over glue poses problems	not compatible: cannot iron over soy wax

A NOTE ABOUT RESISTS AND COLOR

Resists don't affect preexisting color on the cloth, but they can influence the ways that colors integrate as the layering process proceeds. Note the color that is already on the fabric before covering it either partially or completely with a resist. If your strategy includes overdyeing fabric once a resist is applied, review the notes on dye and color on page 20. Neighbors on the color wheel (analogous colors) are always a safe choice for overdyeing. Complements (the opposites on the color wheel) are riskier, but experimenting with them is worth it, so bolster your courage and go for it!

Discharging over a resist shares potential pitfalls with discharging in general. If you haven't made samples and therefore don't know what color to expect from a chemical reaction, you could be in for an unpleasant surprise—or a challenge, depending on your philosophy. It takes some time to apply a resist and wait for it to dry, and that's time and effort invested in the process. Honor yourself and test for color first. It will prevent disappointment later.

When discharging and resisting is completed, fun with the paints and more color begins. The array of potential color schemes and paint styles weave in and out of the discharged or resisted patterning created thus far, enhancing the printing and providing accents or counterpoints. You'll love the effect when the layered surfaces begin to integrate, balance, and come alive.

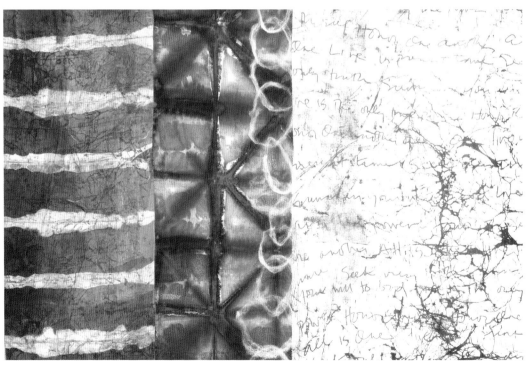

Wax resist was used on left panel and flour-paste resist on right panel.

TROUBLESHOOTING RESIST PROBLEMS

resist fails to completely block dye, paint, or discharge treatment

❖ Did you check to be sure that the resist was fully absorbed, so that no dye, paint or discharge solution could seep under and/or behind it?

❖ Did you allow the resist to dry completely? Removing resist too early can compromise color, pattern, or both.

❖ Was a flour-paste or water-soluble glue resist dissolved by high humidity, either totally or in part? This will compromise line clarity and clean definition of the image. To avoid this disappointment, don't cover resisted and dyed fabric with plastic while batching; air-dry only. There will be enough residual moisture in the cloth to facilitate the reactivity of the dye.

❖ Was fabric with a soy-wax resist immersed in a hot dyebath too soon, melting the wax? Cool the dyebath slightly before adding the cloth.

❖ Did you fail to successfully pair the type of resist with your fabric? Consider fabric weight, type, and coloring method carefully in advance to ensure compatibility. Experiment with a variety of fabric types and textures. Wax penetrates heavier fabrics better than either glue or flour, for example. Discovering which fabrics work best with each of the resists maximizes your use of both time and resources.

Flour-paste resist was used with black textile paint for texture.

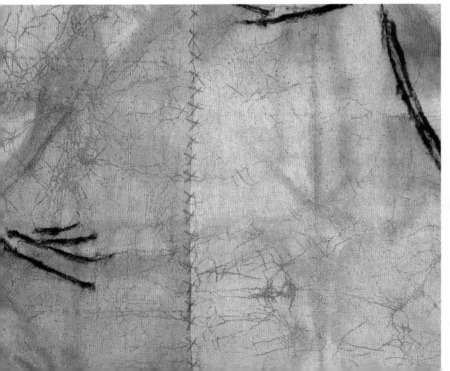

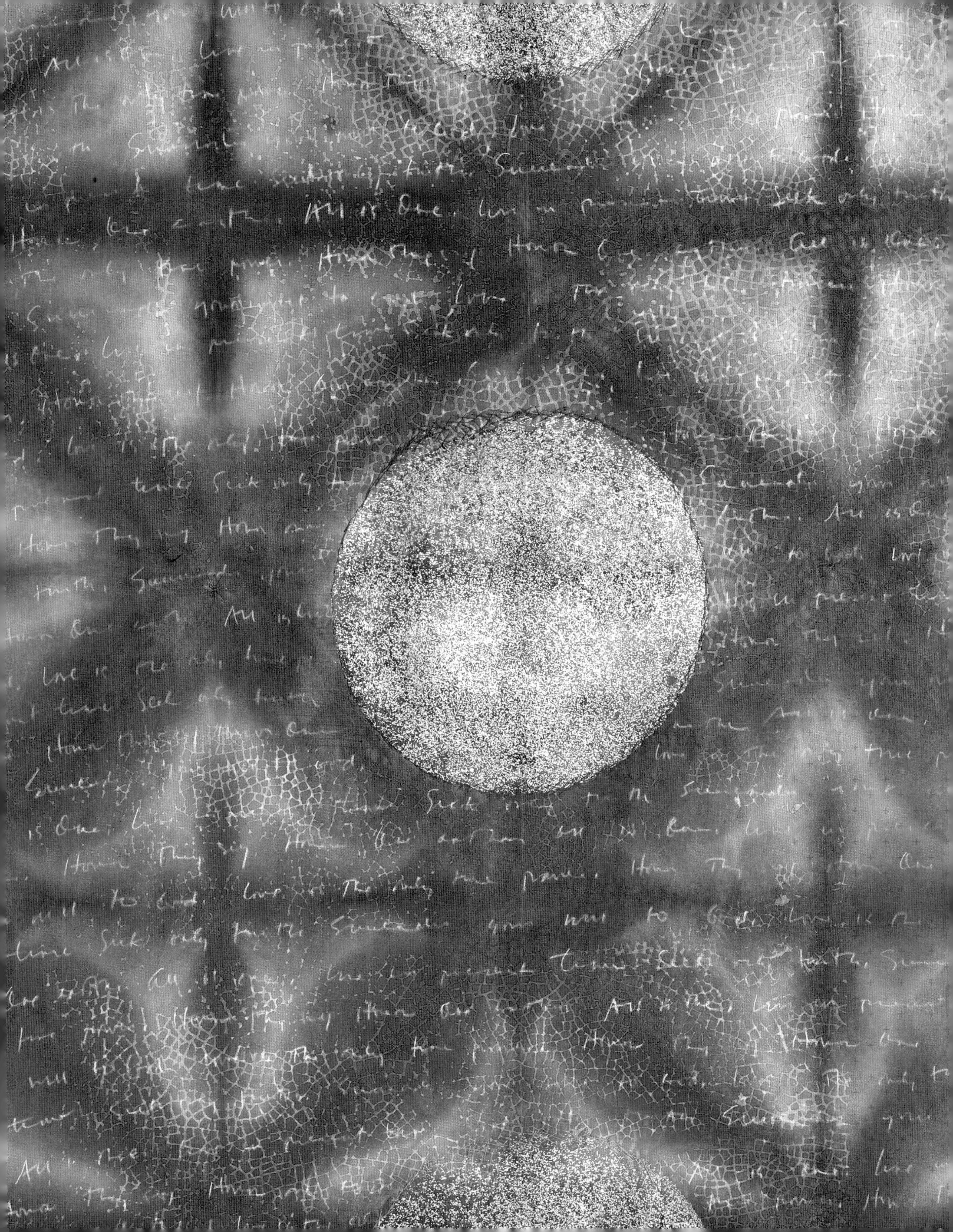
All is One.

print and pattern:
screenprinting

Screenprinting, also known as silkscreen printing and serigraphy, is a modern adaptation of the basic stencil. Europeans experimented with stencils employing silk mesh, attaching it to a wooden frame to keep the fabric taut. This single invention allowed images to be printed in a fraction of the time previously required and led to the evolution of modern-day screenprinting. Screenprinting wasn't considered suitable for "art making" until the late 1940s, when contemporary artists, many of them American, began to explore its potential. In the textile world, incredibly complex patterns have been produced for more than a hundred years in Italy and Germany. William Morris's reputation was built partially on his superb screened patterns, and the home furnishing industry still relies on basic screenprinting processes to create an array of high-end fabrics.

Understanding Screenprinting :: Impermanent Screen Surfaces
Troubleshooting Screenprinting :: Troubleshooting Soy Wax Screenprinting
Permanent Screen Surfaces :: Troubleshooting Photo-Emulsion Screens

Detail, Meditation II, Jane Dunnewold, 2006.
Silk habotai with split dye, Thermofax screenprinting,
Prismacolor pencils, gold foil.

UNDERSTANDING SCREENPRINTING

There are three branches of screenprinting or silkscreening in the world today. The first is printing for commercial industry. Huge facilities exist for production printing with computerized designs and printing processes, using oil-based, water-based, and plastisol inks.

The second branch of screenprinting could be loosely called the traditional approach—that of fine arts programs—rooted in the movement sponsored by the Works Progress Administration in the 1930s and 1940s. In this form, a run of multiple prints is usually produced in an artist's studio, on paper or canvas. Individual screened layers contribute single- and mixed-color combinations to the final print. Oil-based paints and solvents pose potential health hazards, and artists must pay close attention to ventilation and safe practice issues in the studio.

The third branch of screenprinting uses water-based products, including textile paints, so that ventilation and safety issues are less critical. Artists who specialize in fabric printing print with these paints, as well as discharging agents, dyes, resists, and foiling adhesives. This is the type of silkscreening that this chapter will focus on.

Artist William Morris set a new standard of screenprinted textile design.

Works Progress Administration silkscreened poster, 1937. Collection of the Library of Congress, Prints & Photographs Division, WPA Poster Collection. Used with permission.

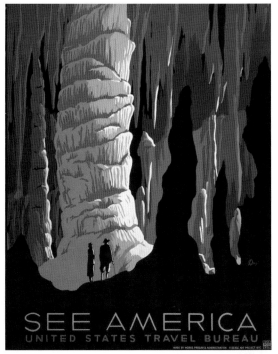

tools and materials for screenprinting

Art supply stores sell traditional supplies, including frames and mesh. Purchase pre-assembled wooden frames without mesh or buy pre-screened, print-ready frames. Some art supply stores sell used frames on consignment at very good prices. Sometimes the mesh cannot be reclaimed, but if you're willing to strip the old mesh and rescreen the frame, used screens represent an excellent value. Supplies are also available online; the Resources section on page 173 is a good place to search for screens and squeegees.

mesh

Although frames were once stretched with silk fabric, polyester or nylon mesh is used on modern screens. Monofilament and multifilament meshes are usually sold by the yard.

- **Monofilament mesh** is very smooth, with no obvious *tooth* or roughness, and is perfect for heavy, viscous oil paint but isn't an appropriate choice for water-based products. Monofilament mesh is always identified by a three-digit number, an indication of thread count; the higher the number, the more threads there are per inch in the weave of the cloth.

- **Multifilament mesh** has more tooth, or roughness, than a monofilament fabric and supports water-based products more effectively than monofilament mesh. Multifilament mesh is identified with a one- or two-digit number, indicating thread count, followed by a series of X's denoting the thickness of the thread used to weave the fabric. An 8xx is a loose weave; a 20xx is a dense weave.

- **12xx mesh** is perfect for most fabric printing because it allows the use of a variety of wet media—from dyes to paints to foiling adhesives—without sacrificing fine detail.

frames

Frames for screenprinting are traditionally made from wood—sometimes oak, which is hard and very sturdy; often pine, because it is inexpensive; and occasionally redwood, which doesn't warp like other wood. Industrial screens are made from aluminum and are sometimes sold in art supply stores.

Reusing a frame when a temporary pattern is removed or washed off is called *reclaiming* the screen. When an image is permanent and the screen cannot be easily reclaimed, you must strip the mesh from the frame and rescreen the frame with a new piece of mesh. For this reason, artists working in home studios should acquire wood frames only, as aluminum frames are almost impossible to rescreen at home.

designs

The goal of a screenprinting application is to block the parts of the screen that are not part of the motif or design element, so paint (or other wet media) can be pushed onto the fabric through the open areas of the screen. Creating a design on the polyester fabric of a silkscreen is called applying a surface to the mesh. The

Silkscreens may be inspired by original designs or clip art. Photocopy your favorites so that you have a permanent image library.

surface application allows wet media to flow through the areas left open in the background on the surface, thus printing the design. Surfaces can be impermanent—designed to print one run and then destroyed, leaving the screen intact for another design—or they can be permanent, allowing for unlimited print runs, as the screen can be cleaned and reused with the same design. Soy wax is unique as a screenprinting surface medium; it can be used to make a surface that is permanent, allowing for many print runs, but it can eventually be washed out, making the screen reusable for a new design.

Classic permanent screen surface applications include light-sensitive photo emulsion and lacquer stencils applied to the mesh with solvent, but there are lots of other ways to generate designs on a screen. Each has unique characteristics and its own distinctive look.

If you intend to experiment with wax or flour paste, visit a thrift store in your neighborhood and look for used electric skillets or hot plates, saucepans, bowls, measuring spoons and cups, and old towels or bed sheets. The value of purchasing used equipment and supplies for your studio goes beyond the dollars saved. We care for the community and the environment when we choose to recycle and reuse as part of our approach to art making.

fabric for printing

The fabric on which you print is critical to the success of both samples and completed pieces. To print samples, use muslin or tear cast-off cotton bedsheets into sample-size pieces. Texture distorts a printed image, so practice on smooth cloth. Working on less expensive fabric at the start provides psychological freedom you won't have if you dive right into the pricey stuff! Eventually, you will want to print on rayon, silk broadcloth, or Pima cotton. See the Resources section on page 173 for companies with wonderful prepared-for-dyeing (PDF) fabrics.

squeegees

The squeegee is the tool used to pull paint across the screen surface for printing. Add several squeegees to your toolbox, even if you use one squeegee for most printing.

It's not necessary for a squeegee to be as wide as the screen. Printing large images with a small squeegee is a matter of practice and experience. Anyone who takes the time to master the technique can do it. Small plastic squeegees and window scrapers are great for printing delicate designs or for printing just a portion of a larger screen. These appropriated squeegees are also better for Thermofax printing, discussed in detail on page 149.

Keep a variety of squeegees and squeegee-like tools in your toolbox.

The best multipurpose squeegee size for fabric printing is less than 12" (30.5 cm) long, with a tapered blade, which will print a variety of media on fabric with precision and ease and is preferable to a square blade. Hunt Speedball makes an inexpensive 9" (23 cm) squeegee perfect for fabric printing and promoted as a textile squeegee.

Squeegees have either wood or plastic handles. Wood-handled squeegees with thick blades are harder to control than smaller, lightweight versions, and are tiring to use. Choose a small squeegee; you'll be able to work longer and enjoy it more.

PROCESS:
ATTACHING MESH TO FRAME AND PREPARING A SCREEN

The simplest way to prepare a screen is to purchase a ready-made screen from an art supply store or from one of the sources listed in the Resources section on page 173. Just tape and wash a ready-made screen as described below. To make your own screen, follow these directions. If you have woodworking experience, make screens with lengths of wood instead of purchased stretcher bars. The frame must be sturdy and square at the corners. These instructions attach the mesh to the frame with staples, but in some cases, purchased frames have a series of grooves around the perimeter of the wooden frame to hold the screen in place; see the sidebar, page 133, for attaching mesh to screens with grooves.

attaching mesh to frame and preparing a screen

1 Assemble the frame by inserting the notched ends of the stretcher bars into one another. Hammer the joins gently until the ends are flush and the frame's corners are 90-degree angles. If the frame is properly joined, the corners will be square and stable.

2 To strengthen the joins, staple diagonally with the staple gun across the seams at corners.

3 Cut the mesh to the size of the frame plus at least an extra 1" (2.5 cm) of fabric all around. Position mesh on the frame so that excess mesh is evenly distributed on each side.

Taped and cleaned screens ready for use.

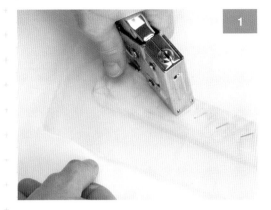

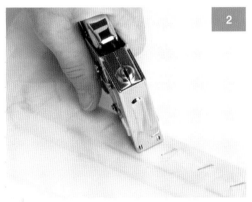

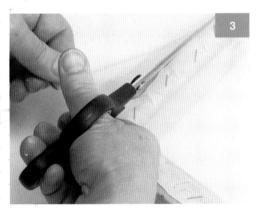

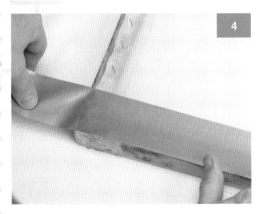

4 The mesh must now be stretched tightly over the wooden frame and attached securely with a staple gun. To staple, start in the middle of the frame's short side. Space staples about 1" (2.5 cm) apart. Staple two or three staples into the frame on an angle **(fig. 1)**. If the staples are vertical or horizontal, the mesh is more likely to tear or develop a run, like a nylon stocking.

5 Pull the mesh taut on the side opposite the first staples. Use the edge of the frame for leverage. Place two or three angled staples into the frame opposite the first set of staples, spacing the staples about 1" (2.5 cm) apart **(fig. 2)**.

6 Continue to staple alternate sides, always stapling on an angle, and stapling the middle of all four sides before completing the corners. This keeps the mesh smooth and taut as it is stretched and allows for greater tension than can be achieved by stapling each side individually. If the staples don't go all the way into the wooden frame, use a hammer to finish sinking them. When you've stapled around the entirety of the frame, use scissors to trim away excess mesh **(fig. 3)**.

7 Whether a screen is pre-stretched with mesh or one you've constructed, it must be washed prior to sealing and taping. Scrub the screen with a grainy cleanser such as Comet or Bon Ami. Dishwashing soap or other cleaners with an oily base are not a good choice for cleaning, as they leave a residue. Allow to dry.

8 When the screen is completely dry, seal the frame with polyurethane. Use a brush to coat the wooden frame with water-based polyurethane sealer. When dry, add a second coat.

9 When the sealer is dry, tape the screen to create the *well*—the place where the paint rests prior to being pulled across the surface of the screen. The tape also prevents leakage where the mesh meets the wood. Use permanent duct tape and tape the screen 24 hours before printing so the tape has time to cure. Properly cured tape won't come off and withstands vigorous scrubbing. To tape, put the tape on the back of the frame (flat side). Cut a piece of duct tape 2" (5 cm) longer than the side being taped. Apply the tape so that it lines up with the edge of the frame. It will overlap onto the mesh. The tape usually covers about an inch of mesh if it's lined up as described. Make sure the tape is smooth and straight **(fig. 4)**. Tape the other three edges on the back the same way.

10 Tape can also be added inside the frame where the mesh meets the frame to keep wet media from building up under the wood. Place the frame right side up. Cut pieces of duct tape the same length as the inside dimensions of the frame. Apply tape to line up exactly with the tape on the back, which is visible through the mesh **(fig. 5)**. The tape on the front and back should extend onto the mesh equally.

11 The tape you applied inside the well area will extend up the inside edge of the frame. Finish taping by smoothing this inside edge and easing the tape into the corners. If wood shows anywhere on the inside edge, add more tape to seal it. Taping takes practice, but you'll get the hang of it by taping a few screens.

12 When printing, if you need to tape off an area of the screen, or need to make a small repair on the mesh, use masking tape. It is less likely to damage the screen surface and makes a strong, but temporary, hold. Always put tape on the back (flat side) of the screen so the squeegee won't pull it off during printing.

Attaching Mesh to a Frame with a Groove System

Some premade screens have a recessed groove system that eliminates staples. A length of cotton cord is required to hold the mesh in place; the cord is pushed down into the grooves with the mesh underneath, so that the mesh is securely anchored. Follow these guidelines:

❖ Cut the mesh 2" (5 cm) wider on all sides than the actual frame measurements. When you use a cord to secure the mesh, extra mesh is needed to accommodate the depth of the groove.

❖ Place the frame with the grooved side facing up. The grooved side is referred to as the back of the screen. Position the mesh on the frame so that the excess is evenly distributed on each side.

❖ Start at a corner and use a screwdriver to push the cording down over the mesh and into the groove. There is a tool called a cord setter that can also be used to push the cord into the groove, but it isn't a necessity; a screwdriver works.

❖ Working across the shortest side of the frame, push down a short section of cording, pulling gently on the opposite edge of the mesh to keep it straight and squared. At the corner, push the cording into the groove around the corner and down the next side. Work around the entire perimeter, alternately pushing cording into place and pulling on the opposite edge of the fabric to keep it square. Once the entire cord is set, run the screwdriver around the entire groove again to make sure the cord is secured as snugly as possible.

If you don't get the screen fabric smooth and taut the first time, just pull the cording out along one edge and try it again. Trim away any excess fabric with scissors when the mesh is satisfactorily set.

- Fabric for printing
- Padded printing table or surface
- Silkscreen prepared with design
- Squeegee
- Textile paint or other wet medium
- Scrub brush

I can't emphasize enough the importance of learning to print properly. A perfect print is clean and crisp, with well-defined edges and little change, if any, in the hand of the fabric. Consistently blurred prints, images heavy with medium, or a slight halo around the printed edges are examples of poor printing technique more than a poor choice of fabric or wet media.

The table surface is very important when you're printing with a screen. Review the instructions for setting up a printing table on page 11. If you don't have space for a large dedicated table, pad a piece of plywood with two layers of felt, staple the felt around the board, and use this surface any time you intend to screen print.

Whether an image can be printed with one pass or not is directly related to the table surface's softness or hardness, the strength of the person printing, the medium being printed, and the fabric. It isn't unusual to need to print several "test" prints to evaluate these variables.

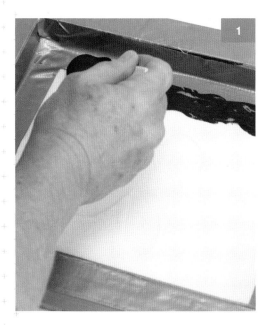

basic screenprinting technique

1   If the screen and image are large, use a Speedball squeegee or an approximate equivalent. If the design is a small screen, Thermofax screen, or delicate image, try a lighter squeegee, a plastic scraper, or even an old credit card.

2   Stand with the screen on the table in front of you at a comfortable height **(fig. 1)**. A surface slightly above waist height is best. My table is 40" (101.5 cm) high.

3   Pour paint (or any wet media) into the well—the taped area—at the top of the screen **(fig. 2)**. Hold the screen firmly with one hand. With the squeegee, pull the paint forward in an even, smooth motion. Avoid pushing and pulling back and forth. Keep the squeegee at a 90-degree angle to the surface of the screen **(fig. 3)**. Don't angle it back or forward; perpendicular to the surface is best, as this stroke efficiently pushes a sheer printed layer through the openings in the mesh.

4   After the paint is pulled across the screen to the bottom, don't push it back up to the top. Instead, scoop it up with the squeegee and deposit it at the top of the screen again. When printing with paint, make sure there is plenty on the screen during the printing process. Keep wet paint flowing across the surface with every squeegee pass, so paint will never dry and ruin the screen.

5   When printing several images at once, images can't be printed consecutively side by side, because wet paint will transfer to the bottom of the screen and leave a ghost image when the screen is repositioned. To avoid the paint transfer problem, screen alternating images and leave space for adding more prints once the first layer of paint has dried, or print randomly across the surface, eyeballing placement.

6   If you must, you can cover damp prints with newspaper to keep the screen frame from resting on wet paint, but take the paper off at the end or it may stick to the dried paint **(fig. 4)**.

7   When you've finished with a screen, clean the screen by washing with cool running water. Use a brush and scrub gently as needed, but don't overdo it. Let the mesh dry completely before continuing to use the screen. A clean screen shouldn't have any residue of paint or chemical left on the tape or inner edges. Sometimes dye or paint tints the polyester mesh. This is confusing because the screen doesn't look clean. Hold a clean screen up to the light and look through the mesh. If you see any opaque areas, wash again to clear the screen completely. Use hot water only as a last resort. Paint that won't wash out cannot be removed; you must cut off the mesh and rescreen the frame.

8   Store screens in an upright position, away from anything that might puncture the surface. Don't stack screens in a pile; they'll warp if not stored upright.

IMPERMANENT SCREEN SURFACES

Impermanent surfaces are designed to print one run. A "run" might include more than a hundred individual prints, but all are made in a single printing session. When printing is complete, the screen is washed, destroying the design in the process but allowing the artist to clean and reuse a screen many times. Paper stencils and flour-paste designs are examples of impermanent surfaces. Soy wax is an impermanent surface because it can be washed out. However, until it's washed out, the surface itself is usable for multiple print runs.

Art cloth by Lisa Kerpoe.

PROCESS:
MAKING AND PRINTING
PAPER-STENCIL SCREENS

Paper stencils are easy to make but can be as complicated as time and ability permit. Any paper can be used to make the stencil, but heavier paper allows the printing of more images, as it takes longer for the paper to soak up wet paint or other media.

making and printing
paper-stencil screens

1 Cut newspaper, newsprint, or oversized drawing paper so the paper is about the size of the blank mesh surface on the screen. If you are using paper that is smaller than the mesh opening, cover any open mesh with masking tape as a temporary block.

2 Use scissors or an X-Acto knife and cutting mat to cut shapes out of the paper **(fig. 1)**. Cut out recognizable shapes or abstract ones. Start with an easy pattern such as a simple flower. You may find it is easier to cut complicated shapes with the X-Acto knife instead of scissors.

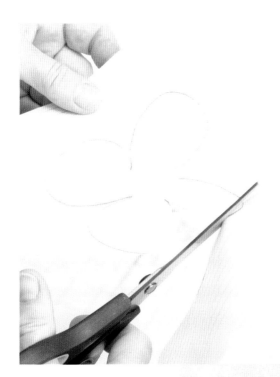

1

3   Another alternative is to cut shapes from the paper and use blue painter's tape to secure the paper to the back of the mesh **(fig. 2)**. The tape holds the paper securely so it won't shift during printing. Always put paper on the back (flat side) of the screen so the squeegee won't destroy it during the printing process **(fig. 3)**.

4   Pin fabric to the worktable to secure it. Use T-pins and pin into the padded surface on an angle to secure the cloth.

5   Place the silkscreen on the fabric. Pour an inch-wide strip of paint along the upper interior edge of the screen. The paint should extend all the way across the well.

6   Use the squeegee to pull the paint across the screen mesh. It may take three or four passes to push enough paint through the open cutouts to produce a crisp, complete print.

7   Lean the squeegee against the inside edge of the frame to stabilize it. Lift the screen carefully away from the fabric by raising the front edge first and check the image **(fig. 4)**. The print should be complete and crisp.

8   Move the silkscreen to a new position on the fabric to make another print. Add paint to the well if you are running out of paint. Replenish paint as you work and use plenty of paint.

9   When the printing session is complete, wash out the screen. Use warm water and a scrub brush or sponge to clean the screen.

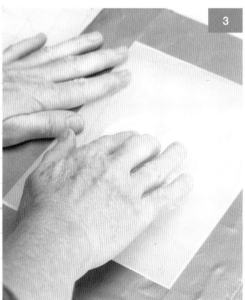

PROCESS:
MAKING AND PRINTING
FREEZER-PAPER SCREENS

Freezer paper is a heavy paper that's coated with plastic. It makes a terrific temporary stencil; it's easy to cut, and the plastic surface keeps it from breaking down as fast as newsprint or copy paper. Available at grocery stores, freezer paper can be ironed temporarily onto screen mesh.

Freezer paper makes attaching separate shapes to the mesh a snap. Save all of the paper cutouts that accumulate as designs are cut. Combine positive and negative elements in two print runs. For instance, print the background first. After the paint and the screen dry, attach the other shapes to the mesh by ironing them in place and then print in a second color. Combining positive and negative elements automatically integrates a design because two versions of the same pattern or motif are represented.

SUPPLIES

• Freezer paper
• Scissors and/or X-Acto knife with #11 blade and cutting mat
• Iron
• Clean silkscreen
• Masking tape or painter's tape
• Padded printing surface
• Textile paint or other wet medium
• Squeegee
• Scrub brush

making and printing freezer-paper screens

1 Cut the freezer paper to fit the opening on the blank screen.

2 Cut out motifs or design elements with the scissors or X-Acto knife.

3 Iron the freezer paper to the padded tabletop to flatten it out. Peel it off the table, turn it over so the shiny side is facing up, and put the blank silkscreen on top of the paper so you can see the shiny side of the paper through the open mesh.

4 Use an iron on medium setting to press inside the silkscreen frame **(fig. 1)**. The goal is to heat the shiny plastic of the freezer paper, adhering it to the screen mesh. It's easier to iron inside the frame than to iron on the raised back of the frame. If the frame is too small to allow the iron to fit inside it, fold a towel and put it inside the frame to support the ironing. Be careful. The polyester mesh withstands considerable heat, but if the iron is too hot, you may accidentally melt the fabric.

5 Once the freezer paper adheres to the mesh, add masking tape around the edges to keep paint from leaking out or underneath the paper **(fig. 2)**.

6 Proceed with printing and cleaning.

PROCESS:
MAKING AND PRINTING
FLOUR-PASTE SCREENS

Flour-paste screens are temporary but resilient, allowing several hundred prints before the surface disintegrates. The scratchy, irregular lines characteristic of this screen surface have an appealing organic quality.

making and printing flour-paste screens

1 Put 1 cup (237 ml) of flour in the mixing bowl. Add ¾ cup (177 ml) of cold water to the flour and stir with the wooden spoon. Continue to add water gradually to the flour, stirring to mix as more water is added. There isn't a right or wrong consistency to the flour mixture, but the easiest consistency to use is slightly thick, like pancake batter. Runny paste doesn't coat the screen evenly. Thick paste makes a surface that cracks easily during printing, which is problematic. Make sure all the lumps are mixed out of the paste. Adding water gradually helps to eliminate lumpiness.

2 Protect the table with newspaper or plastic. When the flour paste is a smooth consistency, apply it to the back of the screen. Pour a 2" (5 cm) wide line of flour paste along one edge of the taped screen **(fig. 1)**.

3 Use the squeegee to smooth the flour paste across the mesh with even pressure. Don't push down too hard or the flour paste coating will be too thin. The goal is to spread a smooth, even coating of flour paste over the entire mesh surface, with no lumps and no open spots **(fig. 2)**. Work up to the taped edges all the way around the screen. If there is leftover paste once the squeegee is pulled across the mesh, put it back in the bowl. If there is paste on the tape when you finish pulling the squeegee, it will wash off later.

4 Allow the flour paste to dry and keep the screen flat, with plastic or newspaper underneath. A fan positioned to blow on the wet surface speeds drying time. Do not dry the screen in direct sunlight unless wide cracks on the dried surface are desirable. The cracks may look great printed, but the uneven drying time contributes to an unstable surface likely to break up during later printing.

- 1 cup (237 ml) white flour
- Measuring cup
- Mixing bowl
- Wooden spoon
- Water (1 cup [237 ml] or more, based on desired consistency)
- Clean silkscreen taped with duct tape at least 24 hours in advance
- Plastic or newspaper to protect your work surface
- Squeegee
- Wooden skewer
- T-pins
- Muslin or cotton sheeting
- Padded printing surface
- Textile paint or other wet medium
- Scrub brush or sponge
- *Optional:* Electric fan to speed drying
- Masking tape

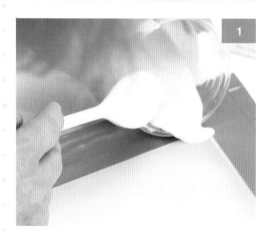

1

5 Wash the tools. Excess flour paste keeps a day or two in the refrigerator, but won't last any longer, so mix only the amount needed for the number of screens being coated.

6 Dry flour paste is a matte, opaque beige color. Thick paste takes longer to dry than thin paste. In either case, it is a good idea to give the screens 24 hours to dry.

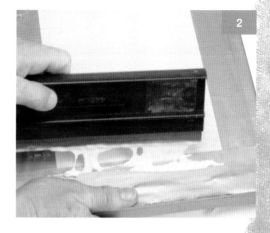

7 When the flour paste is dry, use a wooden skewer to scrape a design into the dried paste on the back of the screen **(fig. 3 and fig. 4)**. Work carefully with the skewer until you are comfortable with the amount of pressure needed to open a design in the dried flour surface. Too much pressure on the skewer punctures the mesh; this can be repaired temporarily with tape but can't be fixed permanently, so be careful.

8 Pin the fabric to the worktable. Use T-pins and pin into the padded surface on an angle to secure the cloth.

9 Place the silkscreen on the fabric. Pour an inch-wide strip of paint along the upper interior edge of the screen. The paint should extend all the way across the well **(fig. 5)**.

10 Print as instructed in Basic Screenprinting Technique, page 134.

11 Continue printing with the flour-paste screen until the run is complete, then clean the screen with warm water and a scrub brush. It may take some scrubbing to remove all of the paste. Sometimes it's possible to save a flour-paste screen for a second run of printing if the flour paste has been on the screen surface for more than two weeks. Seasoned flour-paste surfaces can be sponged clean with cool water and then dried carefully. The screen may still degrade slightly, but that's acceptable as prints always change as paste deteriorates.

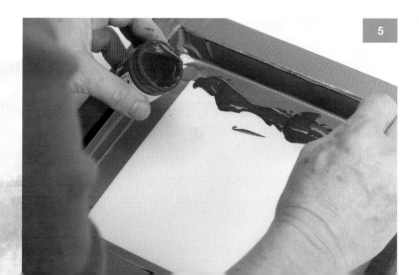

TROUBLESHOOTING SCREENPRINTING WITH IMPERMANENT SCREEN SURFACES

image is incomplete

- Did you use enough paint?
- Was the paint squeegeed evenly across the surface?
- Did you keep even pressure throughout the printing stroke?
- Was the surface under the fabric uneven? Consider making a printing table or use felt under the samples when printing.

printed image is blurred or smeared

- Did you use too many squeegee passes, forcing too much paint onto the fabric?
- Did the silkscreen shift slightly during printing? Steady the frame with the hand that isn't holding the squeegee.
- Was a back-and-forth motion used to print? Always pull the squeegee toward you.
- Is the table padding too soft? Switch to firmer padding or use less padding.

paint prints along the taped edge of an image

- Does the tape fail to cover all of the open mesh along an edge? Add more tape.
- Is the tape failing to stick, so paint slides underneath at the edge? Add more tape.

flour paste is difficult to squeegee onto mesh

- Is the paste too thin? Add flour and stir to remove lumps.

flour paste crackles too much as it dries and lifts away from the screen mesh

- Was the paste too thick at the start? Next time add more water.

flour paste slides into the marks you've made and fills them up

- Was the paste thoroughly dry before scraping into it?

flour paste disintegrates slowly during printing

- Is this the right process for your desired results? With flour-paste screens, every print is slightly different from the ones before it. The paste cracks as the squeegee is pulled over it, so later prints in the run have a crackly background that didn't exist at the start. This is a positive feature of the process, so work with it instead of fighting it.

ART CLOTH

PROCESS:
MAKING AND PRINTING SOY-WAX SCREENS

Apply hot soy wax to a blank silkscreen. Wax is durable and permits hundreds of prints. It's permanent on the screen surface until it's deliberately washed or ironed out, classifying this as a semipermanent screen surface.

making and printing soy-wax screens

1 Screen should be properly taped, clean, and dry. Cover the worktable with plastic or newspaper to protect the surface from wax drips or use a dedicated tabletop.

2 Melt the soy wax in the electric skillet. Turn the heat to a low or medium setting. Watch the wax carefully and never walk away from melting wax.

3 If you're using a hot plate and saucepan (simulated double boiler), pour two inches of water into the saucepan. Put the coffee can in the saucepan of water. The wax melts in the coffee can, and the double boiler keeps the wax from overheating. Work in a well-ventilated area and use a fan to keep fresh air moving.

4 When the wax is melted, turn the temperature dial on the hot plate or skillet down to the warm setting. You can always turn it up again if the wax begins to cool, but it's safer to work with the setting as low as possible.

SUPPLIES

• Clean silkscreen taped with duct tape at least 24 hours in advance

• Electric skillet dedicated to wax process or hot plate with old saucepan and empty clean coffee can

• 1 pound (454 g) or more of soy wax

• Plastic or newspaper to protect your work surface (or a melamine worktable)

• Single-edge razor blade

• Squeegee

• Muslin or cotton sheeting

• Padded printing surface

• Scrub brush

• Rubber or latex gloves

• Synthrapol or Ivory Liquid dish soap

• *Tools for wax application:* Old bristle brushes of various widths, tjanting tool, pieces of natural or synthetic sponge, crumpled plastic wrap or newspaper

Soy wax defines areas of color while isolating and intensifying them.

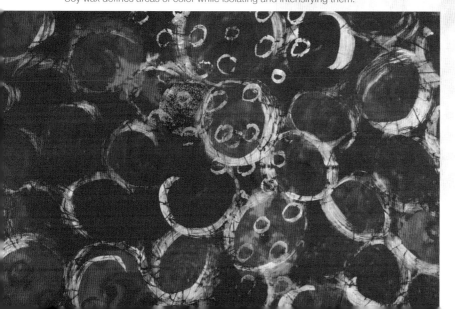

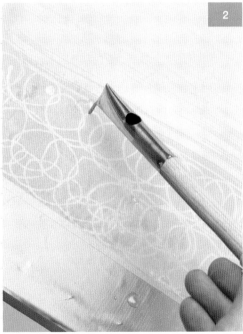

5 Apply wax to the inside or back of the screen, whichever is easier for you. The screen shouldn't be flat on the table, or wax will transfer to the table. Some people find it easier to apply the wax if the screen is slightly angled or upright **(fig. 1)**.

6 Use a brush, a Tjanting tool, or a sponge to apply the hot wax. Tools begin to cool as soon they are removed from the wax pot, so work in small sections and work quickly **(fig. 2)**. If you're using a brush or a tjanting tool, put the tool in the hot wax while it's melting and lean it against the edge of the container for a minute or two. Wrap a rubber band around the handle to prevent it from sliding into the wax pot. Heating the tool brings it to the temperature of the wax and keeps the wax workable longer.

7 The places wax is applied are the parts of the design that don't print. The most effective design is one where the amount of space covered/ waxed on the mesh is almost equal to the amount of open design left to print. Once you've mastered the application process, you'll have a clearer idea of how much wax to add.

8 When hot wax is applied it may run through the mesh, creating raised drips on the other side of the screen. When you've finished applying the wax, use a single-edge razor blade to shave off tops of the drips so the surface is level. The screen is ready to use as soon as the wax cools.

9 Using T-pins, pin the fabric into the padded surface on an angle to secure the cloth. Print as instructed in Basic Screenprinting Technique, page 134.

10 Continue printing with the wax screen until the run is completed. If you wish to preserve the screen, clean it with cold water. If the run is complete and the screen is ready to be cleared, scrub it with hot water and a tablespoon of Synthrapol or Ivory Liquid dish soap. You can also use a hot iron and old newspaper to remove the wax. Put several thicknesses of newspaper on a counter or on your ironing board. Place the screen on the newspaper, with the back flat against the paper. Put additional paper inside the screen frame. Set the iron on high and press over the newspaper, inside the frame. The wax will melt onto the newspaper. Change paper frequently and iron until the wax is absorbed into the paper. Paper with soy wax ironed onto it can be recycled since the wax is biodegradable. Don't put the paper in the trash!

11 Wax screens should be reserved for wax use only. Applying other surfaces to mesh that has previously had a wax application may fail because wax residue prevents other finishes from adhering.

TROUBLESHOOTING SOY-WAX SCREENPRINTING

Practice and experience will help you enormously in controlling soy-wax applications.

wax is runny and difficult to control

❖ Is the wax too hot? Turn down the temperature and let it cool.

wax thickens and begins to cool, making it difficult to handle

❖ Is the wax too cold? Turn up the temperature and give the wax a few minutes to liquefy.

wax runs out of the tjanting tool before you're ready to draw

❖ Are you holding the tool correctly? Hold the tool upright so the wax stays in the reservoir. Holding the frame upright instead of working flat on the table may also help. Tip the tjanting when you are ready to release the wax.

More Ideas for Soy-Wax Screenprinting

❖ Use a pencil to draw the initial design, especially if positive and negative space is hard to envision.

❖ Change tools on the same surface for a variety of textures and scales.

❖ Wax screens are, by their nature, organic. Use them to create background or textural interest.

❖ Be bold when you apply the wax. If you don't like the design, it's easy to iron out the wax and start again.

PERMANENT SCREEN SURFACES

A permanent screen design works with all media from water-based resists to textile paints.

A permanent screen surface is any application that isn't temporary and can't be removed easily, including screens made with acrylic paint and with the photo-emulsion process. Screens with permanent surfaces have several advantages—they're tough, they last for years, and they're compatible with a host of wet media.

Permanent surfaces make it possible to print unlimited runs because the screen can be cleaned and reused. Permanent finishes are ideal for delicate or detailed patterns because the design is generated one time, but can be kept forever. Removing a permanent surface involves cutting off old mesh and rescreening the frame. It's easy to do and should not deter you from generating permanent surface screens.

types of permanent screen surfaces

These processes allow you to create designs on screens that will last for years, if the screens are cleaned and stored properly. Store clean, dry screens vertically to keep the frames from warping and take care to protect the meshes from punctures or stretching.

acrylic-paint screens

Painting a design onto a screen with acrylic paint makes a very versatile surface that accommodates every medium, including chlorine bleach products. Acrylic paints (also called latex paints) are water-based paints in a polymer or plastic base; they clean up with water but dry to a permanent finish.

thermofax screens

The Thermofax machine was originally manufactured to produce master stencils for mimeograph copies; today, they offer a means of generating quick, inexpensive screens from photocopied images. Because they were discarded when photocopiers became popular, used Thermofax machines are still discovered in school and business storage warehouses and are sometimes available through Internet auction houses. New machines are sold by Welsh Distributing Company and Guenther Panenka. See the Resources section (page 173) for services that will generate Thermofax screens for you.

photo-emulsion screens

Photo emulsion is the only method, other than a Thermofax, capable of producing a photographic quality image on a screen. Although the preparation sounds intimidating, it's an easy system to master, and a light unit is a worthwhile addition to any studio.

The emulsion is prepared, applied to the screen, and allowed to dry. A design is photocopied onto a clear transparency (acetate) and then attached temporarily to the screen. The screen is exposed to a bright light for a specific time period. The areas of emulsion exposed to the light harden; the areas protected by the design on the transparency do not. After exposure time has elapsed, the silkscreen is sprayed with a high-powered hose, and the parts of the design that didn't harden wash away.

PROCESS:
MAKING SCREENS WITH ACRYLIC PAINT

This simple process begins with selecting a design and transferring it onto mesh with a pencil or fine-line marker, then using acrylic paint to fill in the background around the pencil lines. An acrylic-painted screen is durable and versatile, allowing you to print paint, thickened dye, discharging agents, or adhesives without risking surface disintegration.

SUPPLIES

- Blank silkscreen, washed and taped 24 hours in advance
- Pencil or fine-line marker
- Any color of leftover latex house paint, acrylic paint in tubes, or water-based craft paint sold in hobby stores
- Assortment of brushes for use with acrylic paints
- Newspaper or plastic to protect the work surface

making screens with acrylic paint

1　Determine the design. This is a great process for overall patterns such as small dots, checkerboards, and hatch marks; it's equally good for line drawings **(fig.1)**. Keep the first pattern simple until you've gauged your tolerance for painting around shapes and filling in backgrounds.

2　Draw on the inside of the screen with the back flat against the worktable. If using a marker, put plain newsprint underneath the screen so the marker doesn't rub off on the table. Newsprint also makes it easier to see the design while drawing on the mesh. When you are pleased with the design, turn the frame over, with the back facing up.

1

Acrylic paint screens have an appealing *woodblock-print* quality.

3 Begin painting the acrylic paint background on the back of the frame **(fig. 2)**. Use a small, fine-tipped brush to paint narrow or interior sections of the pattern first. Apply paint to every part of the background area that requires the fine-tip brush. Work from the inside of the design to the outside edges so you won't get paint on your wrist if it touches the mesh **(fig. 3)**.

4 Now use a wider brush to paint latex paint onto the open areas of the background. You can apply paint so that every bit of mesh is filled with paint, or apply paint unevenly. An uneven application permits pinholes to remain open and the resulting print has an appearance reminiscent of a wood-block print. Check the paint's ability to cover the mesh by holding the frame up so you can look at it with better lighting **(fig. 4)**. If you see pinholes of light, there are still places where paint could leak onto the fabric during printing. This is not necessarily bad, but it is a design choice.

5 Allow paint to dry thoroughly. Since the paint is applied to a fabric surface (the mesh), it should be heat-set. Put parchment paper inside the frame covering the mesh and iron carefully for 30 seconds, keeping the iron moving. The screen is now ready to use.

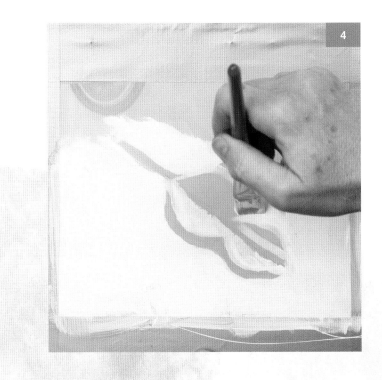

PROCESS:
MAKING THERMOFAX SCREENS FOR SCREENPRINTING

Thermofax machines have an opening about 10" (25.5 cm) wide, into which the Thermofax film, layered with a photocopied design, is inserted. The photocopy must be created using carbon toner. The film/photocopy combination passes through the machine in less than 30 seconds and is exposed to a very hot, bright light inside the machine, melting the plastic coating of the film onto the carbon toner. When the paper/film sandwich exits the machine and the paper is pulled off, the image is transferred to the film and is ready to use. No other method of generating a screen is so immediate.

SUPPLIES

- Thermofax machine
- Plastic Thermofax frames, available in several sizes
- Thermofax film (a polyester mesh bonded to a thin layer of plastic; the plastic side is shiny)
- Design that was printed on a carbon toner photocopy machine (see Step 1)
- Scissors
- Acetate carrier (available from the same sources as Thermofax film) or 11" x 17" (28 x 43 cm) sheet of copy paper

making thermofax screens for screenprinting

1 Photocopy original or copyright-free artwork such as clip art or black-and-white drawings as a carbon toner copy **(fig. 1)**. Most commercial copiers use carbon toner systems. Ink-jet and other types of computer printers are not carbon toner systems. The Thermofax machine will produce an image that looks like the photocopy original; it can be a finely detailed image. The image should fit within the Thermofax frame, with at least one inch of space around the design when placed in the frame; reduce the photocopy image slightly if necessary.

Thermofax machine.

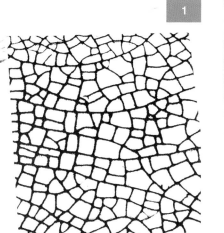

1

2 Cut Thermofax film so that you have a sheet large enough to cover the opening on the plastic frame **(fig. 2)**. The film must extend onto the plastic frame around the opening so it can be securely attached.

3 Put the film on top of the photocopy with the shiny side facing the photocopy. Put the film/copy sandwich inside an acetate carrier or use an 11" x 17" (28 x 43 cm) piece of copy paper as a guide: fold one end of the paper over about 2" (5 cm) and secure the sandwich at the edge of the paper prior to inserting it into the machine. The carrier keeps the two layers together and properly aligned.

4 Insert the carrier into the opening in the Thermofax machine **(fig. 3)**. The machine's roller helps pull the carrier into the machine. The light inside flashes on, and then the carrier exits through a slot at the base of the machine.

5 Open the carrier and remove the copy/film sandwich. The carbon should be bonded to the plastic surface of the film. Separate the film and photocopy by peeling them apart; this pulls the plastic off and opens the design to make printing possible **(fig. 4)**.

6 Tape the Thermofax film to the plastic frame. Use duct tape for permanency. Cut a piece of duct tape the length of one side of the film. Tape the film over the inside opening of the plastic frame. Position the tape so that it overlaps the mesh along the frame edge by about ½" (6 mm), which helps keep the squeegee from cutting the film accidentally during printing. Tape all four sides of the film to the plastic frame using the same method **(fig. 5)**.

7 When the tape cures (about 24 hours), the screen is ready to use.

8 After printing, wash it gently with a sponge and cool water. The screen should last for hundreds of printings.

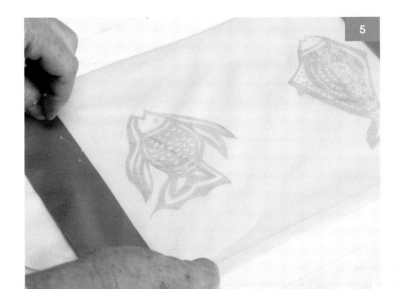

PROCESS:
MAKING PHOTO-EMULSION SCREENS FOR SCREENPRINTING

Photo emulsion is sold as a two-part formula meant to be mixed just prior to preparation of the screen. Choose Diazo photo emulsion over Bichromate emulsion, because Diazo can be mixed and stored several months in the refrigerator. The emulsion is a combination of sensitizer, which is the light-sensitive part of the formula and a carrier, which thickens the emulsion so it spreads evenly over the mesh.

You can use sunlight to expose a photo-emulsion screen, but it's tricky and unreliable. It's easier to set up a simple light unit capable of exposing small- and medium-size screens, as detailed on page 153.

Prepare a drying room in advance of prepping the screen so that the screen can dry without being exposed to light, once it has been coated with wet emulsion. Make sure there is enough time to apply the emulsion and then expose the screen within a 24-hour period; if you allow more time to elapse between coating and exposing the screen, it may not expose properly. See page 154 for information about testing for proper exposure time.

SUPPLIES

- Clean multifilament silkscreen, preferably new, washed and taped with duct tape at least 24 hours in advance
- Diazo photo emulsion
- Plastic spoon
- Squeegee
- A room that can be totally darkened while the emulsion dries
- Four wooden blocks or coffee cups (all the same height) to elevate the screen while the emulsion dries
- Electric fan
- Light source (see page 153)
- Artwork for the screen, printed on a clear acetate transparency
- Glass, cut to fit inside the screen
- 1 yard (91.5 cm) of black felt
- Hose with power-spraying capacity
- Sponge
- Scrub brush

making photo-emulsion screens for screenprinting

1 Prepare a drying room. The screen must dry flat so the wet emulsion won't run. Set up four wood blocks (or substitute four coffee cups or tumblers of the same height) to support the four corners of the screen. Direct a fan toward the blocks to speed drying time. Make sure the blocks are placed so that they support the wood frame and won't touch the wet mesh **(fig. 1)**. Turn off the lights in the drying room. It must be totally dark.

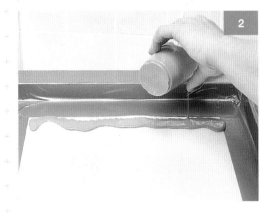

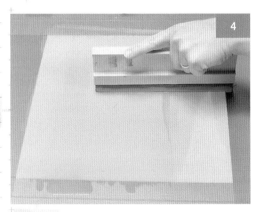

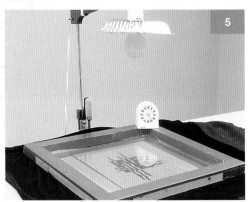

2   Mix the emulsion and sensitizer according to the package directions. Emulsion keeps in the refrigerator for several months. Mark the date on the container with a permanent marker.

3   Apply emulsion in a room with ambient light. Limited exposure to light will not compromise the process, but work quickly.

4   Elevate one end of the screen and pour a thin stream of emulsion along the inside upper edge of the screen, where the mesh meets the tape **(fig. 2)**.

5   Use the squeegee to pull emulsion across the mesh. Squeegee in one even motion **(fig. 3)**. Stopping part way runs the risk of creating a break in the surface. Don't let the coated screen drop and touch the table or your fingers. Anything that touches the wet emulsion will remove it from the mesh.

6   When emulsion is smoothly coated on the mesh inside the screen, turn it over and squeegee the back **(fig. 4)**. The goal is to work the emulsion into the mesh on both sides. The emulsion may look as though the coating is uneven, with some areas being lighter or darker than others, but as long as the surface is completely covered the uneven coloration is unimportant.

7   When the mesh is completely coated with emulsion, transfer it to the drying room. Elevate the frame on the blocks to dry. Turn on the fan. The back of the screen should face down. If any drips of emulsion dry on the screen, it's better if they're on the back against the table during printing.

8   Drying time can be as little as one hour. The screen can also be left overnight. The surface is dry when it's matte instead of shiny.

9   While the screen is drying, set up the light source (see page 153).

10 When the emulsion is dry, move the screen to the light source. Put the screen on top of the black felt facing up. Place the transparency inside the frame, on top of the dry emulsion surface. Place the transparency exactly as you want it when it's printed. Be careful not to reverse the image.

11 Put the glass on top of the transparency to ensure complete contact between the screen surface and the transparency. Turn on the light and set the timer **(fig. 5)**. Determine exposure time in advance by using the testing process described on page 154.

12 When the exposure time is completed, use the high-powered hose and cold water to spray the screen and open the design **(fig. 6)**.

13 Start at the top of the screen and spray across the surface from top to bottom until the unhardened remnants of emulsion dissolve and wash away. If the screen was properly exposed, every part of the design should rinse clean, even minute details. Always use cold water to open a screen design, as hot water can damage the surface even if it was properly exposed. The emulsion is fragile when new. Once it's dry, it's more durable. Cure for 24 hours before printing.

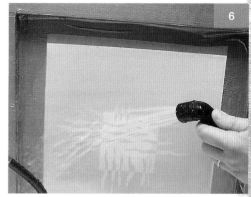

Photos, figs. 1–6: Brent Kane.

PROCESS:
SETTING UP A LIGHT SOURCE FOR PHOTO-EMULSION SCREENPRINTING

The required 250-watt BBA photoflood bulb is available from photography supply houses; no other bulb should be substituted for the 250-watt BBA. A household 100-watt bulb is not as bright as the photoflood.

setting up a light source for photo-emulsion screenprinting

1 Position the clip light so that it is 12" to 18" (30.5 to 45.5 cm) above the surface where the screen will rest during exposure. You can clip the light to a kitchen table leg so that it is 12" to 18" (30.5 to 45.5 cm) from the floor, clip the light to an open closet door, build a wooden stand, or scavenge an old floor lamp from a thrift store. The goal is to attach the light in an upright position, extending over a flat surface where the screen will rest during the exposure time.

2 Pad the area under the light with the black felt.

TESTING EXPOSURE TIME FOR PHOTO-EMULSION SCREENS

- Clean multifilament silkscreen, preferably new, washed and taped with duct tape at least 24 hours in advance
- Black construction paper
- Diazo photo emulsion
- Plastic spoon
- Squeegee
- A totally darkened room for drying the emulsion-coated screen
- Four wooden blocks (all the same height) to elevate the screen while the emulsion dries
- Electric fan
- Light source, as described on page 153
- Glass, cut to fit inside the frame
- 1 yard (91.5 cm) of black felt
- Hose with power-spraying capacity
- Sponge

A photo-emulsion screen can fail because it's either overexposed or underexposed. An overexposed screen results from leaving the screen under the light source too long. The overexposure hardens the emulsion uniformly, and areas blocked by the design on the transparency won't open during the wash out. If the exposure time isn't long enough, emulsion washes off and details of the design may be lost. Emulsion brands and lighting units vary. Test the timing on the unit you build to safeguard against disappointment later.

testing exposure time for photo-emulsion screens

1 Cut the black construction paper to the width of the screen mesh and the length minus two inches.

2 Coat the screen with photo-emulsion solution according to directions on page 152 and allow it to dry in the darkened drying room.

3 Set up the light unit according to the directions on page 153.

4 When the emulsion is dry, position the screen under the light source on top of the black felt with the screen facing up. Put the piece of black construction paper inside the frame, on top of the emulsion surface. The paper should cover the emulsion from side to side, while leaving a 2" (5 cm) exposed area of emulsion at one end. Position the glass on top of the construction paper so that it is held securely against the emulsion-coated surface.

5 Turn on the light and set the timer for 2 minutes.

6 When 2 minutes have elapsed, turn off the light and move the construction paper so that an additional inch of emulsion is exposed to the light. Set the timer for 1 minute and turn on the light.

7 When the next minute of exposure time has elapsed, turn off the light and move the construction paper again, exposing an additional inch of emulsion to the light. Set the time for 30 seconds and turn on the light.

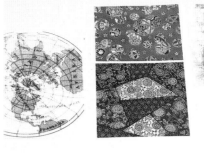

8   Repeat this process three or four more times. Every time the construction paper is moved back on the emulsion, the previously exposed areas are exposed for a progressively longer period of time. Keep track of the total accumulated exposure times. When you are finished exposing the screen for incrementally longer periods of time, you will be able to determine exactly how long a screen needs to be exposed to your light unit, based on the results of the final wash out.

9   Once the series of exposures is completed, apply a blast of cold water to the screen from the high-powered hose. Spray the screen until emulsion no longer washes off the surface. There should be a large area of open mesh, contrasted with a clean-edged, hardened area of emulsion.

10 Check the notes made during the exposure process for the appropriate duration of time for exposure of screens, using the light unit's distance and brightness as determinants.

11 Testing proceeds quickly and is the only assured method for determining proper exposure time. Note the distance from the bulb to the screen surface and the appropriate time for exposure and keep those variables constant every time a new screen is exposed.

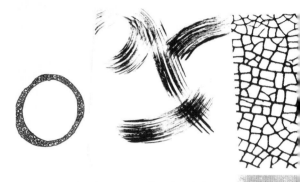

The photocopies above are challenging choices for photo emulsion. They will expose properly, but only with close attention to exposure time. The photocopies on the below will be easier to expose because they exhibit clear black-and-white (positive and negative) contrast.

TROUBLESHOOTING PHOTO-EMULSION SCREENS

The photo-emulsion process is easier than it looks, but it does take a little practice. Check these hints if you have difficulties.

emulsion washes off

❖ Was the exposure time too short?

❖ Was the screen mesh not properly cleaned prior to exposure?

❖ Was the wrong mesh stretched on the frame? Diazo photo emulsion is best matched to multifilament silkscreen fabric.

emulsion won't wash away to open the design

❖ Was the exposure time too long? Reduce the time the screen is exposed to light and try again. Use the test process described on page 154 to accurately determine correct exposure time.

flaws in the design

❖ Are there pinholes or other minor flaws in the surface? These can be repaired by painting fresh emulsion over them. After the emulsion dries, expose it to the light for 10 minutes to harden the repaired surface.

CHAPTER 8

metallic treatments:
foiling and leafing

Metallic foils and leaf add depth, brilliance, and textural interest to dyed and printed fabrics. These high-contrast accents are best added at the end of the layering process because each is susceptible to damage from the caustic properties of soda ash and discharge agents. In addition, neither foil nor leafing products are absorbent, hindering any further use of textile paint or resists. The application process for both accents is the same, but the visual qualities differ, so it's useful to know how to use both leafing and foils.

Foiling :: Applying Foil to Fabric :: Applying Foil with Fusible Web
Applying Foil to Fabric with Adhesive Powder :: Troubleshooting :: Metal Leafing
Applying Metal Leaf to Fabric :: Applying Metal Leaf with Fusible Web :: More Troubleshooting

Detail, Leaf Sampler, Jane Dunnewold, 2007.
Silk broadcloth with dye, discharge, Thermofax
screenprinting, and gold foil.

FOILING

Foils aren't really metal at all. Sheets of foil for textile applications have a shiny surface made of plastic that is bonded to a layer of clear cellophane. The cellophane is peeled away after the foil has been adhered to the fabric. Foils are available in a wide range of colors and patterns, including holographic and rainbow versions.

Materials for foiling and leafing.

foils

Foils are sold by the sheet or by the roll. Sheets can be reused until the foil is completely gone from the cellophane, unless the foil discolors while it is being subjected to heat—a sign of damage. Since the foil is actually plastic, not metal, heat it carefully. Use an iron with a Teflon soleplate for foil application, since the foil can melt and stick to the iron. Foil also has a shelf life; store it in a cool place and discard it if begins to peel away from the cellophane backing indiscriminately.

Foil is sold in an array of colors, but the base for all colors other than gold, copper, and silver is silver foil, to which a sheer layer of color coating is added. If the iron temperature is too high during application, the colored coating breaks down and separates from the silver base, so watch the iron temperature closely to prevent this separation from occurring.

fabrics for foiling

Fabric choice also plays a role in the success of foiling. Silk charmeuse, China silk, rayon, and combed cotton are all excellent choices for foiling, because the smooth, even surface of the cloth facilitates a smooth foil application. Fabrics with an obvious texture can be foiled, but the application won't be smooth and even; the fluctuations in the fabric surface remain visible. This isn't necessarily a bad thing, just another quality of the process to consider when fabric is selected.

Always prewash new fabric prior to foiling. If you've previously dyed or discharged the fabric or printed it with textile paint, the earlier processes must be stabilized before proceeding with the foiling. Foiling should be one of the final steps of layering, since any further dye and discharge processes would strip the shininess from the surface.

Fabrics ready for foiling as final layer.

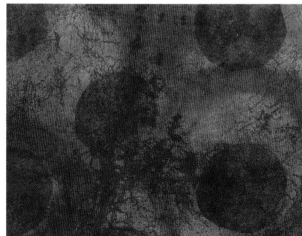

ART CLOTH

adhesives for foiling

Foils can be applied with glues or with fusible web or powder. The adhesive is applied first, in the shape or pattern desired, followed by foil. Instructions follow for both procedures. Foiling with glue is the more versatile option, as it can be applied in any pattern using stamps, stencils, screens, or other methods.

foiling with glue

Glues applied to fabric to adhere foils must be *water soluble*—while the glue is wet, it will wash out with water. Solvent-based glues require paint thinner or turpentine for cleanup, which can be hazardous to your health and to the tools you're using. Read the label if in doubt. If the directions say water will remove the glue as long as it's still wet, it's an appropriate product for fabric foiling.

Though water-soluble when wet, the glue must be permanent when dry. This is very important if the foil is intended for functional use and will be cleaned frequently. Glues designed for use on paper, such as Elmer's Glue or Sobo, are not good choices for foiling. If the fabric gets wet, the glue will dissolve and the foil will wash off. Screen Trans Development Corporation developed the original foils for fabric, and the company sells a good adhesive for this purpose. My favorite adhesive, however, is thick gel medium, sold in art supply stores. Choose a gel thicker than those that can be poured out of the bottle and thick enough to hold a stiff peak on its own. I use products sold in wide-mouth containers, labeled Heavy Gel Medium, Heavy Gel Gloss Medium, and Heavy Matte Medium. Don't thin adhesives with water; this limits the ability of the adhesive to adhere the foil.

methods for applying glue

All of the printing methods discussed in this book are appropriate to foiling. Glues can be applied with stamps, stencils, appropriated tools, Thermofax screens, silkscreens, or by handpainting with brushes. Working with various methods of printing glue for foiling allows you to see what works best for different situations and fabrics. Stamping, for example, prints the sheerest layer of glue on the cloth and may not make a complete print. If the glue image isn't complete, the foiled image won't be complete. Stenciling provides greater control over the application, but screenprinting with a silkscreen or Thermofax screen provides the greatest control and results in the most consistent and even application of all methods.

For a very light adhesive application on sheer fabrics such as chiffon, try applying glue directly to the back of the foil sheet, using a stamp, stencil, screen, or brush. Wait for the glue to dry and then cut out the individual images. Iron them onto the cloth one at a time.

fusible web or powder for foiling

Foiling with fusible web is another alternative. Fusible web is essentially a sheet of heat-sensitive adhesive that melts when ironed. Designed to adhere two layers of fabric together, it can be adapted to foiling. Fusible adhesive powder can be sprinkled across the cloth and then foiled to achieve the effect of a light glitter dusting on the fabric.

caring for foiled fabrics

Foils are stable after it's adhered with a permanent adhesive and the cellophane is removed. Iron foiled areas with a pressing cloth to protect the sheen. Wash foiled fabric in a washing machine and line-dry the cloth. You may also be able to spot dry-clean a foiled fabric, but take a sample to the dry cleaner first. Just as sequins are stripped of color by some dry-cleaning fluids, foil can lose its sheen if improperly handled.

- Fabric

- Heavy gel medium or other water-soluble glue that is permanent when dry

- *Tools:* Stamps, stencils, silkscreens, Thermofax screens, brushes, or appropriated tools

- Iron with Teflon soleplate (or use a pressing cloth with a regular iron)

- Foil

- Hard, padded surface, such as a table or countertop with felt padding

Test foil on several fabric samples while you're learning the process and see how each responds. Remember that glue is permanent when dry; if the fresh printed images aren't satisfactory, wash the fabric immediately to remove them and start over.

applying foil to fabric with glue

1 Fabric should be dry and stable. Iron the fabric to remove wrinkles.

2 Apply the glue using one of the following methods:

Brush adhesive onto a stamp with a small foam brush and apply it to the fabric **(fig. 1)**.

Apply glue through a stencil, using a stencil brush, or a small foam roller **(fig. 2)**. Make sure the glue is evenly distributed on the roller to avoid printing some areas of the fabric more densely than others.

Silkscreen the glue onto the fabric **(fig. 3)** or screen it through a Thermofax screen.

Handpaint glue onto the fabric. Select a brush size to fit the scale of the lines or dots or swaths of adhesive you intend to make. Heavy glue applications change the hand of the cloth dramatically, so practice to achieve a light touch with the brush.

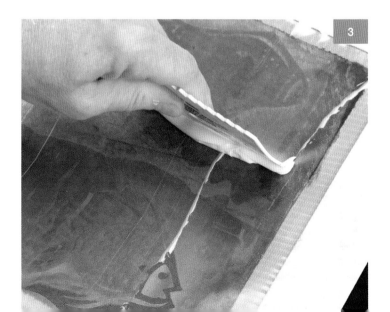

3   Allow the glue to dry completely before applying foil. It may take more than an hour for the glue to dry, so be patient.

4   Working on a hard, padded surface, such as a table or countertop with felt padding, set the iron on high heat. Medium isn't usually hot enough, but you may want to test this in advance on a sample. If the iron doesn't have a Teflon coating, use a pressing cloth to avoid melting the foil.

5   Apply the foil with the hot iron one small adhesive area at a time **(fig. 4)** using the technique described in Step 6. Don't cut the foil up; use a large sheet, as it is easier to press than small bits. Repeat the foiling process until the glued image is covered.

The cellophane layer is the top and is fused to the colored side of the foil! To keep this straight, my foiling mantra is: *See the color*. It's easy to get confused and turn the foil color side down. You must *see the color* to ensure correct orientation of the foil sheet.

6   Use the side of the iron up near the tip to apply the heat **(fig. 5)**. This detail is critical. The foil glue softens if too much heat is applied, and putting the iron down flat on the foil often melts it. Use the side or tip of the iron to scuff firmly across the foil. Push away from your body and count to four as you iron; that should be long enough for adhesion.

7   Peel away the cellophane **(fig. 6)**. If the fabric isn't foiled evenly, and glue is still exposed, reapply foil and heat again.

PROCESS:
APPLYING FOIL TO FABRIC WITH FUSIBLE WEB

- Fabric
- Fusible web
- Scissors
- Iron with Teflon soleplate (or use a pressing cloth with a regular iron)
- Foil
- Hard, padded surface, such as a table or countertop with felt padding

Choose a lightweight fusible web over a heavier version, to avoid changing the hand of the fabric. I prefer the MistyFuse brand of fusible web, but Wonder Under is another great choice. Lighter fusibles won't change the hand of the fabric.

applying foil to fabric with fusible web

1 Cut a shape from the fusible web **(fig. 1)** and place the web on the fabric. If the web has a paper backing, apply the web to the fabric, then remove the protective layer before foiling.

2 Cover the web with foil, color side up.

3 Heat the foil with the iron. This step is a bit different from dried glue. The fusible takes a longer time to melt, so carefully place the iron on the foil and press back and forth until the fusible is melted **(fig. 2)**. Keep the iron moving so the foil does not melt.

4 Allow the foil to cool. When cool, peel away the cellophane **(fig. 3)**.

5 If the foiling isn't even, reapply in the areas needed.

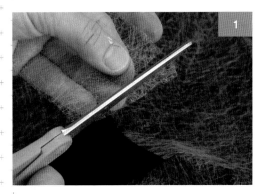

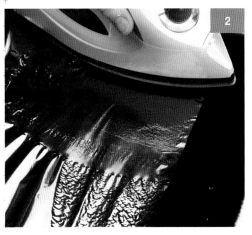

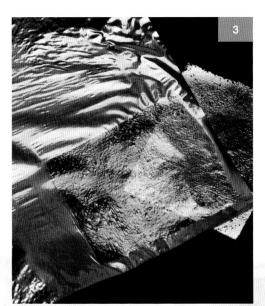

Completed foil application.

PROCESS:
APPLYING FOIL TO FABRIC WITH FUSIBLE ADHESIVE POWDER

With fusible adhesive powder as the base, foils give the effect of a light glitter dusting on the fabric. Experiment with this method to achieve varying degrees of subtlety or drama.

applying foil to fabric with fusible adhesive powder

1 Sprinkle fusible adhesive powder on the fabric.

2 Place foil over the adhesive on the fabric, color side up.

3 Heat the foil with the iron. This step is like using fusible web. The fusible powder takes a longer time to melt, so carefully place the iron on the foil and press back and forth until the powder is melted. Keep the iron moving or the foil may melt.

4 Allow the foil and fabric to cool; otherwise the fusible powder will pull away when the foil is lifted.

5 Once the foil and fabric have cooled, peel away the cellophane.

TROUBLESHOOTING FOIL APPLICATION PROBLEMS

Successful foiling takes practice; experiment with different types of glue, iron temperature, and pressing surface to get a feel for the technique. This list of troubleshooting tips may help you remedy common errors.

foil washes off

❖ Did you use the correct type of adhesive? Make sure your choice is permanent when dry.

❖ Was the iron hot enough? Try a higher setting.

foiling fails

❖ Was the glue application too light? Stamping and handpainting run a risk of too light a touch; try another method of adhesive application.

❖ Was the glue thinned with water? This weakens its ability to hold the foil.

❖ Was the glue too thin? Choose a thicker product.

❖ Was the iron hot enough? Up the temperature and try again.

Metal leafing looks similar to foil but is a very different product. Leafing has a lower sheen and subtle appearance. As with foil, though, its general purpose in the layering process is to provide accent or contrast.

choosing metal leafing products

Metal leaf, or leafing, is sold in several forms. The most common and least expensive leafing material is a *composition metal leaf*. This product doesn't have a very high percentage of expensive metal content, but it's reasonably priced and can give beautiful results. Composition metal leaf is sold as silver or aluminum, copper, or variegated colors with a gold, silver, or copper base. Gold leaf in 22-karat and 24-karat weights is also available, but expensive—reserve gold leaf for special projects.

In the United States, metal leaf is sold in packages of flat individual sheets, called *pages*. There

are twenty-five pages of leafing in a pack. The pages are 6" (15 cm) square, so one package of leaf covers a 24" x 48" (61 x 122 cm) section of fabric if the leaf is applied uniformly over the entire surface. If you apply the leaf as an accent on the cloth rather than an overall surface, one packet of leafing may be enough to do a much larger or longer length.

using metal leafing on fabric

Plan to add metal leaf when the fabric embellishment is near completion. I cut the package of metal leaf into sections with scissors. If I'm working on a piece of fabric that requires long, thin strips, I cut through the entire set of sheets, leaving the paper between the composition metal pages. Cutting the "book" of sheets into smaller components saves leaf in the long run, because I use only what I need and little is wasted.

All metal leaf is fragile; imagine a hair-thin sheet of metal. While foiled fabric can actually be washed in a washing machine, leafing is more fragile than other surface treatments and should be handled with care. If leafing is intended for functional cloth, as in the creation of a garment, be judicious in use and placement of imagery. Leafing can handle limited dry cleaning if properly applied. Metal leafing is stabilized when the leafing is applied and the adhesive is dry. No other effort is required to ensure the permanency of the application.

adhesives for metal leafing

Both heavy gel medium and fusible web are suitable for adhering metal leaf. Fusible powder isn't a candidate for metal leafing because it wastes so much leafing. Use foil if the project at hand requires metallic "dust" to be complete.

Metal leaf adds light and resonance to any fabric surface.

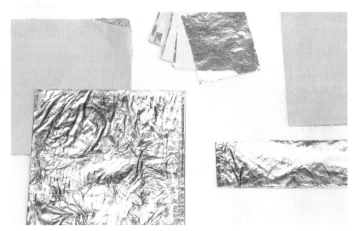

Leafing is sold in sheets, booklets, and as loose fragments.

PROCESS:
APPLYING METAL LEAF
TO FABRIC WITH GEL MEDIUM

Just as with foiling, the most reliable adhesive for a leafing application is thick gel medium, sold in art and craft supply stores. Choose a gel that won't "pour" out of the bottle. I recommend the thickest products, which are sold in wide-mouth containers and labeled Heavy Gel Medium, Heavy Gel Gloss Medium, and Heavy Matte Medium. A heavy application of gel medium will change the hand of the cloth, so practice getting just the right amount. There must be enough gel to sit on the surface without sinking in, but not so much gel that the fabric is stiffened from the coating. Do some sampling on fabric that already has several layers of dye, printing, or other treatments.

applying metal leaf
to fabric with gel medium

1   Fabric should be dry and stable. Iron to remove wrinkles.

2   Apply the gel medium with the tool of choice **(fig. 1)**. Work quickly and wash tools immediately, as the gel medium is fast drying and permanent when dry.

3   Allow the gel medium to dry completely; this is likely to take one to four hours depending on application method and atmosphere/environment.

4   When the gel is dry, position a piece of leaf slightly larger than the area of dry gel on top of it. Cover with parchment paper. Press with a dry iron, using the flat of the iron, to ensure a good bond **(fig. 2)**.

5   Use a soft cloth or brush to brush away the excess leaf **(fig. 3)**. Brush unused fragments into a plastic bag or envelope and save for later use.

6   Dull the shininess of the leaf by brushing across the surface, abrading it with the paintbrush.

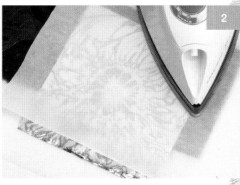

APPLYING METAL LEAF TO FABRIC WITH FUSIBLE WEB

SUPPLIES

- *An assortment of metal leafing products:* Composition gold, silver, or copper metal leaf, and/or a composition leafing packets that feature oxidized swirls of red, blue, green, or black coloring
- Fabric
- MistyFuse or other fusible web product
- Scissors
- New 2" or 3" (5 or 7.5 cm) soft natural bristle paintbrush
- Parchment paper
- Hard, padded ironing surface
- Iron

Fusible web is a sheet of heat-sensitive adhesive that melts when ironed. Designed to adhere two layers of fabric together, it can be adapted to metal leafing. Choose a lightweight fusible over a heavier product to ensure softness of the hand. I prefer MistyFuse, but Wonder Under is another good choice.

applying metal leaf to fabric with fusible web

1 Cut your desired shape from the fusible web. If the web has a paper backing, apply it to the fabric, then remove the protective layer before foiling.

2 Place the fusible web on the fabric and cover it with metal leaf. Cover the leaf with parchment paper.

3 Heat the leafing with the iron **(fig. 1)**. This step is a bit different from applying leafing with gel medium. The fusible web takes a longer time to melt, so carefully place the iron on the parchment covered leaf and press until the fusible web is melted. Metal leaf won't burn, so there is no need to keep the iron moving. Allow the leaf to cool.

4 Once the fabric cools, brush away the excess leafing with the soft brush **(fig. 2)**. Save larger pieces for later use.

Art cloth with metal-leaf treatment.

TROUBLESHOOTING METAL LEAF APPLICATION PROBLEMS

Metal leaf is a precious tool; don't be afraid to practice with it but address any errors with these tips.

leafing washes or rubs off after the initial application

❖ Was the gel medium too thin? Never thin gel medium.

❖ Was the application of gel medium thick enough to ensure coverage?

❖ Was the iron hot enough?

❖ Was the texture of the fabric disruptive to the bond between gel and leafing? If using a rough or textured fabric, test first to be sure the leafing and cloth are compatible.

Considering Color with Foil and Leaf

Choose foil or leaf color based on the color scheme developed on the length of cloth. Gold foil or leaf is spectacular on warm backgrounds such as yellow, orange, and red. Silver leaf or foil is a good choice for cool colors such as green, blue, and purple. Copper is a great choice for red or rust fabrics and is striking paired with blue or green.

Though metal leaf is sold in a limited palette, the leaf can be tinted with textile paint.

Use a cotton ball to apply a small amount of paint, rubbing it gently into the surface. Wait for a minute and then remove excess paint with a clean cotton ball. A hint, or blush of color, will remain.

Adding paint to leaf creates these artistic effects:

❖ Black paint over gold leaf gives a bronzed appearance.

❖ Blue or green paint over copper leaf looks oxidized.

❖ Green over gold looks oxidized.

❖ Black paint over aluminum or silver leaf looks like pewter.

Metal leafing can be tinted with textile paint.

appendix

Pure Dye Colors and Weights in Grams	
color	weight of one level teaspoon of dye, in grams
Sun Yellow 108	2.64
Lemon Yellow 114	4.20
Tangerine 112	1.17
Golden Yellow 104	4.31
Strong Orange 202	2.66
Burnt Orange 515	2.26
Pro Mixing Red 305	2.80
Strongest Red 312N*	3.44
Fuchsia 308	2.86
Boysenberry 802	4.23
Grape 801	3.20
Basic Blue 400	3.61
Intense Blue 406	2.52
Pro Mixing Blue 402c	3.20
Deep Navy 414	2.81
Turquoise 410	1.17

Identifying numbers are those used by PRO Chemical & Dye and are current at publication.

*Not a pure dye

Volume/Fluid Measurements

cup	fluid ounce	tablespoon	teaspoon	milliliters
			1/4 tsp.	1.25 ml
			1/2 tsp.	2.5 ml
			3/4 tsp.	3.7 ml
			1 tsp.	5 ml
	0.5 fluid oz.	1 tbl.	3 tsp.	15 ml
⅛ cup	1 fluid oz.	2 tbl.	6 tsp.	30 ml
¼ cup	2 fluid oz.	4 tbl.	12 tsp.	59 ml
⅓ cup	2⅔ fluid oz.	5⅓ tbl.	16 tsp.	79 ml
½ cup	4 fluid oz.	8 tbl.	24 tsp.	118 ml
⅔ cup	5⅓ fluid oz.	10⅔ tbl.	32 tsp.	158 ml
¾ cup	6 fluid oz.	12 tbl.	36 tsp.	177 ml
1 cup	8 fluid oz.	16 tbl.	48 tsp.	237 ml
2 cups	16 fluid oz.	32 tbl.	96 tsp.	474 ml
4 cups	32 fluid oz.	(1 quart)		946 ml
16 cups	128 fluid oz.	(1 gallon)		3,800 ml (=3.8 liters)

volume
1 gram water occupies 1 milliliter = 1 cubic centimeter
1000 ml = 1 liter

length
1 inch = 2.54 centimeters (cm)
36 inches = 1 yard = 0.9 meter (m)
100 cm = 1 m = 39.4 inches

weight
1 ounce (oz) = 28.3 grams (g)
16 oz = 1 pound (lb) = 454 g
2.2 lb = 1 kilogram (kg) = 1,000 g

temperature
212°F = 100°C = boiling point of water at sea level
32°F = 0°C = freezing point of water at sea level

HOW TO DYE A COLOR WHEEL

SUPPLIES

- ½ yard (45.5 cm) fabric
- One-gallon bucket
- Measuring cup
- Measuring spoons
- Scissors
- Pen and masking tape to label cups
- 12 containers, such as yogurt containers or plastic cups, about one-cup size (237 ml)
- Hot water
- Soda ash
- Salt
- *Optional:* Gram scale, Edwards's book or another color wheel for reference, card stock, and glue stick
- Fiber-reactive MX dyes (identifying numbers are those used by PRO Chemical & Dye Co.)
  - 108 Sun Yellow
  - 202 Strong Orange
  - 305 PRO Mixing Red
  - 312N Strongest Red (not a pure color)
  - 802 Boysenberry
  - 801 Grape
  - 400 Basic Blue

Dyeing a color wheel provides another tool you can consult at a glance as colors are determined for lengths of cloth. The foundation of creating art cloth is using the color wheel, memorizing colors and dye recipes, and combining that information with immersion and printing methods.

The basic twelve-color wheel includes three primary colors (yellow, red, and blue); three secondary colors (orange, green, and violet); and six tertiary colors, each of which is a combination of one primary color and one secondary color. Red-orange and blue-green are examples of tertiary colors. All other colors are derived from these twelve colors.

My goal in designing this exercise was to develop formulas for the twelve-color wheel colors using available pure dyes. Fewer dye colors in a formula translates into fewer opportunities for dye to split or strike in unexpected ways. I based my color matching on a color wheel printed in Betty Edwards's book *Color: A Course in Mastering the Art of Mixing Colors* (Tarcher/Penguin, 2004), but any commercial color wheel is an equally good place to begin.

Through testing, I discovered that many of the pure colors are exact matches to color-wheel colors. The exceptions are red and green. The pure red dyes available to the dyer have a blue overtone, so none of them is suitable as a match to the color-wheel primary red. I mix two red dyes together to get the color-wheel primary red. Green is also not available as a pure dye, so the green in my recipes is a mixed color, generated from a pure yellow (PRO Chemical & Dye #108) and a pure blue (PRO #400). Colors look slightly different on different fabric types. I use silk noil for one set of colors and cotton batiste for the second set so I could compare them.

A dyed color wheel in my dye journal.

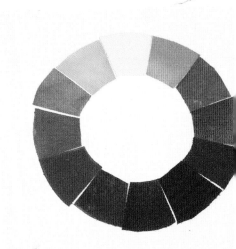

FIBER REACTIVE MX DYES
ON SILK NOIL

YELLOW: SUN YELLOW #108

ORANGE: STRONGEST
ORANGE #202

RED: EQUAL PARTS PRORED
305 AND STRONGEST RED
312N *

RED-VIOLET: BOYSENBERRY
#802

PURPLE: GRAPE #810

BLUE: BASIC BLUE #400

* Strongest Red is not a pure color, but as there is no pure red dye that is the color wheel red. I used a 50/50 mix of 305 PRO Red and 312N Strongest Red. This combination produces an effective color wheel red.

GREEN: A pure green dye does not exist, so this color must be mixed. I used a combination of 108 Sun Yellow (8 PARTS) and 400 Basic Blue (2 PARTS) to match the color wheel in the Edwards' book

how to dye a color wheel

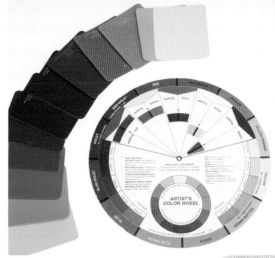

1 Mix the water/salt and soda ash chemical water by combining 1 gallon (3.8 liters) hot water, ⅓ cup (79 ml) soda ash, and ½ cup (118 ml) salt. Dissolve chemicals completely. If you are making dyebaths for yardage, you will need a larger quantity of water. Keep the proportions the same per gallon, if increasing the chemical water recipe.

2 Dye solutions are made from chemical water and dry dye powder. **Colors for the color-wheel dyeing are mixed from these dye solutions.** For each dye color, mix dye solution by adding 1 teaspoon dry dye (or equivalent gram weight) to ⅔ cup (158 ml) chemical water. Dissolve thoroughly. Mix all of the colors in the above list.

3 To dye the samples required for your color wheel, use either a single dye solution or a mixture of two solutions as indicated in the chart on page 172. If a recipe indicates that the color is a mixed color, use the proportions suggested in the chart. Pour colors into 1-cup (237 ml) containers.

4 Cut fabric into twelve equal pieces. Immerse one piece in each of the dye containers.

5 Batch the fabric swatches for three hours in the cups.

6 When batching is complete, empty dye into the sink. Rinse the fabric pieces in cold water. When water runs clear, rinse the pieces in hot water. Rinse by hand to keep the colored pieces straight. Pay attention to which containers pieces came from! Since the samples won't be washed again, it isn't necessary to use Synthrapol or a washing machine. Hand rinsing will remove the migrant dye.

7 Air-dry the samples and press them.

8 *Optional:* Cut the samples into pieces the right size for a color wheel and assemble them on card stock with a glue stick. Label the colors with the proper color name and indicate which dyes were used to create the color for future reference.

I match colors to color chips; a good color wheel is another option.

Dyeing the color wheel makes it possible to match color chips exactly for an invaluable resource.

Suggested Dye Stocks for Color Wheel

color in color wheel	dye solution proportions
yellow (single dye solution)	8 tablespoons (118 ml) Sun Yellow 108
yellow-orange (mixed color dye solution)	8 tablespoons (118 ml) Sun Yellow 108 + 2 tablespoons (30 ml) Strongest Orange 202
orange (single dye solution)	8 tablespoons (118 ml) Strongest Orange 202
red-orange (mixed color dye solution)	8 tablespoons (118 ml) Red (see line 5) + 1 tablespoon (15 ml) Strong Orange 202
red (mixed color dye solution)	4 tablespoons PRO Red 305 + 4 tablespoons Strongest Red 312N
red-violet (single dye solution)	8 tablespoons (118 ml) Boysenberry 802
violet (single dye solution)	8 tablespoons (118 ml) Grape 801
blue-violet (mixed color dye solution)	5½ tablespoons (83 ml) Grape 801 + 3 tablespoons (45 ml) Basic Blue 400
blue (single dye solution)	8 tablespoons (118 ml) Basic Blue 400
blue-green (mixed color dye solution)	Blue Green:5½ tablespoon (83 ml) Basic Blue 400 + 2 tablespoons (30 ml) Green
green (mixed color dye solution)	8 tablespoons (118 ml) Sun Yellow 108 + 2 tablespoons (30 ml) Basic Blue 400
yellow-green (mixed color dye solution)	8 tablespoons (118 ml) Sun Yellow 108 + 3 tablespoons (45 ml) Green

*Color numbers refer to PRO Chemical & Dye products.

resources

While this list is reliable at publication time, I urge you to use a good Internet search engine for terms and products whenever you need more information.

General Supplies

Dharma Trading Company
Box 150916
San Rafael, CA 94915
dharmatrading.com
(800) 542-5227

Dick Blick
Box 1267
Galesburg, IL 61402
dickblick.com
(800) 723-2787

Jerry's Artarama
Box 586381
Raleigh, NC 27658
jerrysartarma.com
(800) 827-8478

Nasco
Box 901
Ft. Atkinson, WI 53538
enasco.com
(click on Arts & Crafts Materials)
(800) 558-9595

PROChemical & Dye Inc.
Box 14
Somerset, MA 02726
(508) 676-3838
(for technical information)
(800) 228-9393 (to order)
prochemicalanddye.com

Screen-Trans Development Co.
100 Grand St.
Moonachie, NJ 07074
(201) 933-7800
screentrans.com

The Silk Connection
Jacquard Products
Box 425
Healdsburg, CA 95448
(800) 442-0455
silkconnection.com

Testfabrics Inc.
Box 26
West Pittiston, PA 18643
(570) 603-0432
testfabrics.com

Triarco Arts & Crafts
2600 Fernbrook Ln. #100
Plymouth, MN 55447
(800) 328-3360
triarcoarts.com

Welsh Products Inc.
Box 6120
Arnold, CA 95223
(800) 745-3255
welshproducts.com

E-mail Lists

Contact individual lists for information on joining.

Complex Cloth
More than 1,000 members share information and advice freely.
complexcloth@yahoogroups.com

QuiltArt List
The Internet's largest mailing list for contemporary art quilters
quiltart.com

Helpful Websites

committedtocloth.com
Claire Benn and Leslie Morgan host this informative site about workshops and events in the United Kingdom.

complexcloth.com
The author's website, with essays, images, and inspiration

entwinements.com
Karren Brito's site always offers something new and interesting concerning shibori and/or dyeing.

fiberarts.com
The website for *Fiberarts* magazine.

pburch.net
Encyclopedic information on dyes and discharging agents

quiltingarts.com
The website for *Quilting Arts* magazine.

Opportunities for Study in Textiles and Surface Design

Crow Timber Frame Barn
nancycrow.com

Houston Quilt Festival
quilts.com

Minnesota Textile Center
textilecentermn.org

Pacific Northwest Art School
pacificnorthwestartschool.com

Quilting by the Lake
quiltingbythelake.com

Studio Art Quilt Associates (SAQA)
saqa.com

Southwest School of Art and Craft
swschool.org

Split Rock Arts Program
cce.umn.edu/splitrockarts

Surface Design Association
surfacedesign.org

The Fine Line Creative Arts Center
fineline.org

Thermofax Services

Contact individual services for information and updates on availability and turnaround time. Search for Thermofax services online for additional providers.

Bobbie Vance: *fiberartBV@aol.com*
Marcy Tilton: *marcytilton.com*
Northwoods Studio:
northwoodstudios.us
Pam Relitz: *rockitz@tds.net*
Su Butler: *subudesigns.com*

bibliography

Later editions of some books are available; these listings are from the author's personal collection.

Allen, Jeanne. *Designer's Guide to Japanese Patterns*. San Francisco, California: Chronicle Books, 1984.

Benn, Claire, Jane Dunnewold, and Leslie Morgan. *Finding Your Own Visual Language*. London: Self-published, 2006. Available from www.complexcloth.com.

_____. *Paper and Metal Leaf Lamination*. London: Self-published, 2007. Available from www.complexcloth.com.

Bothwell, Dorr, and Marlys Mayfield. *Notan: The Dark-Light Principle of Design*. New York: Dover Publications, 1991.

Brackmann, Holly. *The Surface Designer's Handbook*. Loveland, Colorado. Interweave, 2006.

Dunnewold, Jane. *Complex Cloth*. Bothell, Washington: Fiber Studio Press, 1996.

Edwards, Betty. *Color: A Course in Mastering the Art of Mixing Color*. New York: Jeremy Tarcher/Penguin, 2004.

Faine, Brad. *The Complete Guide to Screen Printing*. Cincinnati, Ohio: North Light Books, 1989.

Gilman, Rayna. *Create Your Own Hand-Printed Cloth: Stamp, Screen, and Stencil with Everyday Objects*. Lafayette, California: C & T Publishing, 2006.

Gunner, Janice. *Shibori for Textile Artists*. New York: Kodansha International, 2007.

Hornung, David. Colour: *A Workshop for Artists and Designers*. London: Laurence King Publishing, 2005.

Johnston, Ann. *Color by Accident*. Lake Oswego, Oregon: Self-published, 1997.

_____. *Color by Design*. Lake Oswego, Oregon: Self-published, 2001.

_____. *Dye Painting*. Paducah, Kentucky: American Quilter's Society, 1992.

Joyce, Carol. *Textile Design*. New York: Watson-Guptill Publications, 1993.

Kafka, Francis, J. *Batik, Tie Dyeing, Stenciling, Silk Screen, Block Printing: The Hand Decoration of Fabrics*. New York: Dover Publications, 1959.

Laury, Jean Ray. *Imagery on Fabric*. Lafayette, California: C & T Publishing, 1992.

Noble, Elin. *Dyes and Paints*. Bothell, Washington: Fiber Studio Press, 1998.

Proctor, Richard, and Jennifer Lew. *Surface Design for Fabric*. Seattle, Washington: University of Washington Press, 1984.

_____. *The Principles of Pattern For Craftmen and Designers*. New York: Van Nostrand Reinhold, 1971.

Rossol, Monona. *The Artist's Complete Health and Safety Guide*. New York: Allworth Press, 2001.

Schwalbach, Matilda, and James Schwalbach. *Silk Screen Printing for Artists and Craftsmen*. New York: Dover Publications, 1970.

Stocksdale, Joy. *Polychromatic Screen Printing*. Berkeley, California: Oregon Street Press, 1984.

Waterman, Ann V. *Design Your Own Repeat Patterns*. New York: Dover Publications, 1971.

Wells, Kate. *Fabric Dyeing and Painting*. Loveland, Colorado: Interweave, 1997.

ART CLOTH

index

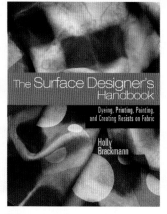